THE FATHER OF VALUE INVESTING
BENJAMIN GRAHAM
A COMPLETE BIOGRAPHY

AF522491

PUSHKAR KUMAR

Published by

PRABHAT PRAKASHAN PVT. LTD.
An imprint of Prabhat Prakashan Pvt. Ltd.
4/19 Asaf Ali Road,
New Delhi-110 002 (INDIA)
e-mail: prabhatbooks@gmail.com

ISBN 978-93-5521-488-1
BENJAMIN GRAHAM: A COMPLETE BIOGRAPHY
by Pushkar Kumar

Edition
2025

Price
₹ 350 (Rupees Three Hundred Fifty only)

Printed at
R-Tech Offset Printers, Delhi

To the "Father of Value Investing" and the man who was responsible to bring a modern wave to the world of investment, Benjamin Graham.

Author's Note

Widely known as the "Father of Value Investing", Benjamin Graham was a British-born American researcher, economist, professor and investor. This book is an attempt by the author to introduce Benjamin Graham and his life to the world. So, that everyone could learn how he became an investing genius and what principles he followed to achieve success.

Benjamin Graham was the former mentor of the renowned investor Warren Buffett. He had many other outstanding disciples who had achieved substantial success in the world of investment, including Irving Kahn, Charles Brandes, William J. Ruane, Bert Olden and Walter J. Schloss. Moreover, he has been an inspiration to all who have ever wished to enter the world of investment.

He is the author of the popular investing book named "The Intelligent Investor". The book is considered the investor's bible. Graham has also written another founding text in neoclassical investing with David Dodd named "Security Analysis." Graham got the inspiration to write the book after the market crashed in 1929. The book helped in laying out the fundamental framework of value investing.

Graham believed that investment is most intelligent when it is most business-like. According to him, buying undervalued stocks, which have the potential to grow over time, is beneficial. For him, an intelligent investor is one who sells to optimists and buys from pessimists.

After completing his studies at Columbia University, Graham started his career on Wall Street. Later, he founded the Graham-Newman Corporation. He earned $ 500,000 annually by the age of 25. Besides his remarkable work in fundamental value investing, he also made many contributions to economic theory. He was responsible to revolutionized the perception and methods of investment in the stock market.

Graham died on 21st September 1976. Though he is now not living between us, but he is still alive through his work. Hopefully, this book will help the readers to know and understand Benjamin Graham better and learn many life lessons.

– Pushkar Kumar

Contents

Childhood in New York

Often, most people remember numerous accounts of their initial childhood. However, Benjamin Graham was not one of them. As a matter of fact, he does not remember many of the incidents that occurred before the death of his father, Isaac M. Grossbaum. Benjamin was eight-and-a-half at that time and therefore finds himself sceptical whether the incidents he remembered were right out of his memory or just the narrations he heard people telling him over the years.

For instance, the incident that he remembered as part of his emotional memory was the enthusiastic voice of his mother, Dora Grossbaum, waking him and his two brothers, Leon and Victor, in the morning asking them to check at the window to see that the 21st century had arrived. He was just five-and-a-half years old then, and the youngest of the three children his parents had. Leon his eldest brother was two years older and Victor, the middle one was a year older. Though in retrospect, he struggled with the facts of the stories he remembered that whether they were actually out of his memory or were just the narrations his mother made over the years.

Born on May 9, 1894 in London, England, at 87 Aberdeen Road, Benjamin Graham's original name was Benjamin Grossbaum. It was when his family moved to New York City in the United States of America the next year, they changed their name from Grossbaum to Graham later in a desire to assimilate into American society and avoid anti-Semitic and anti-German sentiments.

Being attracted to academia since his childhood, the first thing he took upon himself was to know the meaning of his name Benjamin. He searched the 'Bible' to gather information about others having the same name and about their characters and achievements. He found that the name Benjamin comes from the Old Testaments of the Bible where Benjamin is called the 'Apple of his father's eye and much loved by his brother Joseph'. Also, he further found out that the Benjamin mainly did only two things in the story – 1. Cries on Yusuf's neck (45:15), and 2. Procreate children more than any of his brothers, ten children – all sons.

A frequent traveller, as he was in his later years, during one short journey at the age of 61, he felt inclined to revisit his birth place. Upon reaching the place with great difficulty, he found something amiss. He realized he mixed the previous house number, number 14, with his present addresses of Brighton at Cambridge Road and had reached some place he never knew. As his memory served, and as per his family traditions, they lived in a very comfortable house with a beautiful garden with several domestic staff to help them with day-to-day chores. They were paid a monthly salary of £1 each, he remembered. To refresh his memory of his old house, his paternal cousin Wilfred sent him a photograph of his earlier house as he remembered it in the year 1956. He went there again in the year 1960 and found the place quite similar, a pleasant well secured house with a garden that spread on both sides.

Benjamin found the age gap between him and his brothers disturbing as his eldest brother Leon was only about 14 months older than his second brother Victor who was only 13 months older to him. Though, this age gap came with some benefits for the three brothers as they all grew up as a unit, for instance, learning French from their *Mademoiselle* together. It was during this time that Benjamin wrote a letter in French to '*Cher papa et maman*', his parents, while they were on a tour.

Remembering bits and parts of his childhood, Benjamin had a little memory of the number of governesses they had as the only impression of their presence was particularly the way the food was cooked. One of the memories he had was of often having *Charlotte Russe*, a sponge cake filled with whipped cream as a sweet dish or dessert. The memory stayed in his mind because he remembers his *Mademoiselle* cutting the boxes of the popular biscuits, Uneeda biscuits, and moulding them into shapes to keep the cake.

Benjamin Graham's family was in the business of porcelain and figurines that they imported from China, Austria and Germany. His father and grandfather headed the business. The Graham family moved quite a lot because of the business and by the time Benjamin was born, there was a frenzy of changing places of their residence that continued for several years. The Graham family moved their business to London soon after his elder brother Victor was born and then a year later they decided to set up an American branch that was to be managed by his father. Hence, some time in the 1895, almost a year after Benjamin was born, all five members of the Graham family moved to New York. During those days people moving from one country to another did not require immigration documents or any other documents whatsoever.

When the Graham family moved to New York, it was not clear whether or not they planned to settle in America on a permanent basis. Benjamin's father decided to live in a shared accommodation with one Myers family in place of purchasing their own house. His father, Isaac M. Graham was known for his pride in his British Nationality that he kept intact till the time of his demise. It was the time when the British nationals did not want to shift their allegiance to others. Regardless of everything, the Graham family got their American citizenship only after the First World War was over.

Like his father, Benjamin Graham was also known for his staunch patriotism towards his British-hood. However, because of his belief, Benjamin had to face several challenges during his initial years through regular criticism and persiflage. At the turn of the century, there was a strong feeling of inferiority amongst the Americans with regard to the Britain and British people. The British mannerism and grandiosity, British accent, British clothes were all considered ridiculous in American milieu.

The Myers family with whom the Graham family shared their accommodation consisted of a widowed mother and her eight children - four sons and four daughters. As Benjamin's delicate memory serves, the Myers family was very friendly with them, particularly with him being just a small child. However, as he recalls, this friendliness never stopped them from teasing him for being British. Recalling an incident from his memory, Benjamin recounted the story of the boat race of America Cup in which Sir Thomas Lipton, a British merchant and a famous yachtsman, also owner of famous Lipton Tea, participated with his yacht *Shamrock*. Being an articulate child, Benjamin strongly expressed his belief in the victory of Sir Thomas Lipton. However, it never happened and consequently Benjamin became the centre of teasing in the Myers family. The twinge of those scars remained with him for a very long period of time.

It did not end with the Myers' family. As Benjamin started his school, he found his pro-British bias in the face of his classmates' anti-British sentiments. So much so, they even compared George Washington with George the III emphasizing that the former also won the dubious war of 1812. However, his ordeal nearly came to an end when he was about 10 years old when his accent almost shifted from British to American.

While remembering his early childhood, Benjamin recalls a huge picture of the three brothers that was taken in Richfield Springs, New York when he was two years old. However, as he recalls, it was not just one but several of its portrait-sized extensions that were hung on various walls of his house. In the photograph all three brothers were seen standing in descending order from left to right wearing white sailors' uniforms. The amusing part of the memory was that though his brothers were seen wearing shorts in the photograph, Benjamin was shot wearing a short skirt. In those days, it was customary to dress very young boys, who had not reached the age of functional dependence, in skirts, which made it easy for the nurse maids to change garments in case of accidents.

The story behind the photograph was equally interesting. Richfield Springs was considered the fashionable summer resort for the privileged at that time. Benjamin's father had leased a shop to run his business. Though, most of his father's business, as he recalls was carried out through auctions from Saratoga, Bay Harbour, Mackinaw Island and places like Sarvahara Atlantic City. While in Richfield Springs, they were witness to the Annual Richfield Springs Independence Day Parade on July 4, 1896. The three brothers were made to stand on the store window to watch the parade. According to his mother, as Benjamin remembers, they were standing so still and motionless on the window that they gave the illusion of being mannequins.

Though Benjamin questions the actual series of incidences that took place that time, he however recalls that their motionless stance attracted the attention of a professional photographer who offered to click their photograph on the cost of displaying it on the window of his photo studio. The guests at the Graham house used to get ecstatic seeing them in the photograph; however, it took too long for Benjamin to look at that white skirt with an indulgent smile in place of bitter humiliation.

Notwithstanding the fact of how amazing Isaac Graham was, Benjamin sadly regrets that he hardly remembers anything about him. He says that he had only heard a rhapsodic adoration about his father as it was a general consensus that he had a 'heart as big as a world', which he had shown towards his family, parents, siblings and even other people. Apart from being a very attractive, animated and almost always cheerful person, he was also an excellent and very resourceful businessman.

It was during his last years, the British branch of Isaac Graham's business was failing and whatever he profited from his American branch was used for the sustenance of his family, siblings and a substantive army of his nieces and nephews in England.

Isaac Graham's health took a toll owing to the overload of his work. Benjamin accompanied him during one of his tours to Hot Springs, Virginia for medicinal purposes. Though, as Benjamin recalls, he only had three memories of this travel. First was that they had to remain imprisoned in their hotel room for a few days due to spring floods that brought the melted snow from nearby mountains onto the roads. Second was his friendship with the wealthy Swift family who were famous for their meat products and staying at the same hotel. Third was his memory of one Grape-Nuts incident that happened with Benjamin one morning during breakfast.

One morning his mother suggested that he should have his breakfast alone in the dining room as he was grown-up enough to do so. Elated with the confidence his mother had shown in him, Benjamin, who was only five at that time, jumped at the opportunity and sat alone at the table in the dining hall with all his pride reading the menu card. As he recalls, he does not remember whether he read the menu himself or asked the waiter to read it for him, he found himself attracted to a new concept – 'Grape-Nuts', which is a kind of breakfast cereal, and which he was unaware of till that time. Narrating the incident, Benjamin said that he ordered the same for himself. Surprised, the waiter asked him that, "have you eaten it before?" To which Benjamin replied in the negative. The waiter continued saying that he might not like the item and asked him to order something else. Sitting there alone full of pride, it was more or less the question of prestige for Benjamin. He insisted on having only 'Grape-Nuts' and was served the same.

It was the phase in Benjamin's life when his teeth were very sensitive and having Grape-Nuts added fuel to the fire. That wonderful breakfast scraped his teeth like gravel. Trying to being oblivious to the discernible expression of superiority on the waiter's face, Benjamin not only cleaned the breakfast to each and every crumb but spoke a defiant lie of liking his breakfast. As he later said, he never ordered Grape-Nuts after that incident for a very long time.

Another thrilling and memorable experience that Benjamin remembers was his journey to England with his brother Leon. Although two brothers were accompanied by their parents, Benjamin does not remembers his father being part of this memory. In retrospect he recalls that it was probably because his father was part of just dropping and picking them up at the end of their trip. The only memory he has with his father in it was while they were returning back to New York. Being just a seven-year-old boy, Benjamin was quite a favourite amongst the passengers who used to make him stand in front, chin up and made him recite 'Oh Captain, My Captain' repeatedly. So much so that he was invited to the Whitman's Elegy to recite the same during the traditional Captain's dinner that the members of the crew and the passengers organized two nights before the ship touches the port.

The incident remained in his memory as not a fond one because his father refused to send him for the recital saying that he was too young to be awake so late at night and that this kind of attention was not good for such a young child. However, Benjamin found out next morning that his father had not just cancelled his performance the previous night, but instead recited a very long poem at the party himself. The sting of deception remained with Benjamin against his father for a very long time, which later he realized was unfair on his part.

Benjamin treasured this journey to England and bragged about it to his friends. However, there was not much about the trip that he remembered. A few bits and pieces that he remembered were an endless journey from South Hampton to London via train; three of his father's sisters with tennis rackets in their hands which he later found out were gifts from his father to them; and lastly the beautiful garden of his maternal grandparents' house where they all miraculously fitted in for a gathering.

It was in 1901 as Benjamin remembers. Queen Victoria had died a few months ago. Benjamin found himself shocked by the black paint that covered almost all the woodwork in front of the shops there. He remembers being told that Edward the VII was unwell during that summer and therefore his coronation ceremony was postponed.

Benjamin also remembers parading on the road with his brother Leon in a military formation duly wearing short Khaki uniforms and holding wooden rifles as the Boer War was at its peak. He tried to attract attention of the countless soldiers present on the road from atop one of those famous open double-decker Omni buses.

During his England trip, they spent a very short period of time in London and went to spend a major part of their summer in Brighton at his maternal grandparents' house in Gesundhiet's, a huge grey-stoned mansion at 14 Cambridge Road. His maternal grandfather Gesundhit, as he recollects, was a white bearded, fat and delightful man while his grandmother was plump, emotional and a very assertive woman who had recently returned from her visit to Paris and brought bottles full of hard candies for them. His mother's younger sisters – Margret and Caroline were very loving towards the two brothers.

While at his grandparents', Benjamin had a special memory of services in the synagogue. Probably because he comes from a very orthodox family from both sides, he had attended those services on quite a regular basis. Benjamin amuses a procession of Rabbi's five sons entering their pew (a place to sit in the synagogue) in a line all wearing Eton Suits with top hats.

A horrifying memory that Benjamin recalls from his stay with his grandparents was of an accident with the gas heater at the Rabbi's house leaving him suffering with severe burn injuries. The Rabbi was restricted to his room for quite a long time. He remembered visiting him with his family and found the Rabbi all draped in bandages.

The memory of visiting Brighton beach was one of his fond memories of that trip. As he recalls, it was a joy to bathe in the water as the sand was very smooth under the feet. However, the nasty accumulation of pebbles a little further in the water made it torturous for them to walk at the same time. However, Benjamin himself wonders why they were so desperate to go and bathe there in the sea water as the water was cold, the beach was full of pebbles and the surprising part was they didn't know how to swim.

Nonetheless, they found the Brighton bathing machines at the beach very amusing. As Benjamin portrays, the bathing machines were closed wagons used by the bathers as dressing rooms near the water that saved them trips to the shore to change clothes on the pebbled path. They were placed adjacent to each other and were visible during the low tide at the water-core. Several horses were associated with the wagon shaft of every machine and were used to haul them up during the high-tide and back during the low-tide. Recalling one incident that Benjamin considers as a beautiful memory was of the massive storm followed by the flood of waves. It was all so sudden that there was no time to haul the wagons to safety and most of them were carried into the sea by the receding tide. Portraying the memory, Benjamin says the wagons were floating on the sea and the excited assemblage on the shore watched them being hooked with ropes by the seamen from their boats to drag them towards the shore. The two brothers secretly hoped for another big storm and a similar spectacle!

A little before Benjamin took the trip to London with his brother and parents, the Graham family had shifted to their private four-storeyed house at 122nd Street near Seventh Avenue from Myers' boarding house. It was a big house and the Grahams had an Irish help in this house. It was in this house that Benjamin found a new apparatus that he enjoyed fiddling with. It was the Speaking Tube. Also known as a voicepipe, it is a kind of device with two cones connected by an air pipe to convey messages from one room to another. Benjamin used this tube to play and disturb his Irish maid.

Although there were several phases in Benjamin Graham's childhood about shifting from places to places and adjusting amongst different cultures, yet he was a very courteous and composed child and never found himself in trouble for being naughty or mischievous. Similar to him, his eldest brother Leon was known for possessing the most balanced personality of the three brothers. However, his elder brother Victor (the middle one) was a different case. He was the most impish one and was actually considered the troubled child during his adolescent period. So much so, that he had to undergo institutional discipline after which he changed into a better person.

Benjamin remembers going after his mother and father in every room of the house irrespective of the floor. It was the month of April in the Graham house and the *Passover* (a Jewish festival) was round the corner. While following his parents from room to room, he saw his father holding a big feather and an ordinary dustpan, the symbolic tools engaged in the traditional custom called '*Pursuit for Chametz*' on the eve of *Passover*. The house was meticulously cleaned removing every speck of grain used for daily food and his mother took out two sets of utensils reserved for such holy days. Benjamin remembers seeing a massive supply of special stuff that was brought into the house—from tens of pounds of matzoth in large spherical packages; big blue paper cones of extra hard sugar that was to be hammered into coarse pieces and a special supply of milk, jam and condiments. He remembers the festival as some kind of quest to prove their satisfaction or the satisfaction of one very rigid God that there was nothing to breach the tenets of *Passover* in the house.

They soon shifted to another house at 125th Street in Fifth Avenue of 2019 when Benjamin was just five or six years old. This house was a brown-stoned private house with plate-glass windows on the second floor of the house. The Grahams used the parlour behind these windows to showcase their porcelain items. Being very young, the Graham boys were strictly forbidden to enter that area threatened with dire consequence if acted otherwise. However, they were definitely taken on a carefully guarded tour during the inspection.

Reminiscing on his days, Benjamin talked about going shopping with his mother to different places for assorted items. Their usual place was 125th Street, which was considered a very fashionable centre for the high society business during those days. However, their grocery and meat items came from a big market of Weisbaker, whereas for most of the other items they used to visit Coach & Co., an ordinary departmental store. Another of their shopping arcades for big purchases or for a huge selection of items was Bloomingdale on 59th Street, where it remains even today.

It was the time when the subway was still to be constructed and therefore the common mode of transportation, especially to Bloomingdale was a trolley car. The Grahams found the E1 system inconvenient for travelling and automobiles were still a matter of curiosity for the people. Recalling the streetcar system that was most prevalent at that time, Benjamin adds that the streetcar system was quite evolved at that time with several competing and cooperating lines covering extensive inter-car transfers.

Uniformed gentlemen provided these cars sitting under vast umbrellas on various important crossings. What was interesting in Benjamin's anecdote was that these umbrellas displayed big slogans 'all the cars go till Bloomingdale' which became one of the household phrases of his childhood.

Benjamin started his schooling at the age of five in a very reprehensible manner. He went to a nearby communal kindergarten that was situated on the second floor of some building. The only fond memory of those days was sitting cheerfully in front of the box of sand with a huge seashell in it. Admitting a very embarrassing memory, Benjamin said he realized that he would be soon thrown out of there because he was the only child yet to master the difficult art of opening and closing the buttons of his pants. He had to ask the teachers to help him before going to the toilet. After a few days of this annoyance, he added, he was sent back home never to return to that school. Because of all this he was made to wait till he was slightly older and went back to school to start his studies from Class 1 onwards after September 1900 at the age of six-and-a-half years. Another reason for his eager willingness to go back to school was his brothers' attitude towards him who teased him of being a baby staying back home while they went to school.

Benjamin had an intrinsic ability for academics and therefore he proved to be a curious and successful student. Because of his abilities to learn fast and with precision, he was soon promoted to a higher grade. Though good at academics, Benjamin soon realized he possessed scholastic abilities but was below average in the athletic games. He was a healthy boy though somewhat younger than those of his age. He said, though the scholars in those days were not expected to excel in athletics too, yet he was made to participate in games and other exercises. He soon realized that he had poor muscle coordination and hence suffered from general awkwardness. As a result, he was found dropping and breaking things, bumping into them so much so that he got hurt in the process. As if this was not enough, he realized he was terminally delusional, constantly being absent-minded or daydreaming, calling unnecessary attention to him for being lackadaisical.

Due to this, Benjamin was also victim of his brothers' attitudes towards him. He later contemplated that if only he had ever tried to understand the mind of a young boy that might have been captivated by several interesting thoughts that are strange even for him preventing him from paying attention to the physical world around him, then apparently his brothers would have treated him in a similar way as the brothers of young 'Joseph the Dreamer' had treated him.

Another interesting anecdote that Benjamin recalls was of the day their *Mademoiselle* used to take leave. It was the day the three brothers were alone without anyone to supervise them. On one such day, the three brothers decided to visit 65th Street and Fifth Avenue inside the Central Park where a small locomotive used to pull a train for young children. They walked the distance of over three miles on foot just to watch engines emitting smoke and tiny cars making various rounds to and fro. Obviously they were only spectators as they had no money to take a ride. However, the wheels turned in a different direction when they were almost home and realized that it was too late and entirely dark outside.

The three brothers decided to stop for a while to chalk out a strategy as to how to present their misadventure to their parents as the punishment was inevitable. His eldest brother Leon, who was nine at that time, stepped forward and agreed to take the brunt of the situation while the two younger brothers entered the house hiding behind him. The house was tense; his mother and a few others even feared kidnapping or some accident. They had even called the police a while ago.

Remembering the day, Benjamin said both Leon and Victor got what they all feared, heavy punishment. However, he was spared for being the youngest and probably was viewed as the viable tool in his brothers' hands.

Talking about the day, Benjamin muses that the small engines they went to see in the Central Park were used to pull elevated trains during those days. They used to pass over their heads on the elevated tracks thunderously blowing whistles. Even the sparks from their wheels were visible in the dark evenings of winter. He added, later when the electrification of E1 took place, those small steam engines were huddled in a small elevated yard besides the tracks. They were later sold to some South American country, he added.

Remembering those days, Benjamin said that the electrification of New York Central Lines took place quite later at the Park Avenue. The trains used to move in an open cut from passenger bridges smoking steam. His parents used to take him to these bridges when he was four or five years old. He felt delighted seeing those engines coming towards him and then passing from under the bridge he was standing on. The modernization changed the entire scene adds Benjamin, saying that those engines and even those rail roads—that were built on solid steel pillars with intertwined iron structures throwing their shadows on the roads below—have vanished from the scenes of New York today. It seems like they never existed, adds Benjamin. He talks about witnessing various other massive and strong changes in his lifetime. He narrated a few lines of Ronsard that he used to sing during his college days to remember the good old days –

Le temps s'em va, le temps s'em va, ma dame,
Las! Le temps, non, mais nous, nous en allons.
(Time goes by, time goes by, My Lady,
Not the time, Ah! This is us who pass on.)

People go, whereas the time and world continues to remain. This is true, Benjamin muses, even after all this he feels that the world that he knew and the leisure that was the specialty of that less complicated world, is no more—other than his own living memory. A brief existence, still it is him in these many words who had on one hand buried the time and yet kept it alive, irrespective of what Ronsard sings.

❑

Family Tragedies and His Mother's Perseverance

Talking about his family and the events connected to that, Benjamin remembers that their summer tour of England proved to be the most delightful moments of their wealth and happiness for years to come. However, a little later after they returned from England, Benjamin's grandfather Grossbaum died. He remembers receiving this news suddenly through cablegram and his father breaking down inconsolably with the news. Benjamin remembers his father sitting on a Chinese chair with his feet on a footstool wearing an old suit with cut-off sleeves and deliberately broken buttons. This conservative sitting position called 'Sitting Shiva' is an elaborate ritual to mourn one's departed parents.

It was only after 50 years of his grandfather's death that Benjamin found out the dramatic details of his death while wandering on the streets of London with his paternal uncle Sole. His uncle stopped at a corner between Bond Street and Regent Street and said, "We had a store here when your grandfather was alive". He told Benjamin that his grandfather had a trusted assistant who, his grandfather found out was embezzling money from their business. His grandfather threatened to hand the assistant over to the police. The embezzler threatened Benjamin's grandfather with a gun saying, "My life is as such ruined and if I shoot you and am hanged for the crime even that would be better than what is there at present". He then said to Benjamin's grandfather that, "You are a genuine, god fearing Jew. If you swear on the Bible that you will not mention my misappropriation to anyone, I will spare your life". Benjamin's grandfather swore on the Bible and never mentioned the theft to anyone. However, the major financial setback and the shock of threat on his life took a major toll on the old Grossbaum's health and he died of pneumonia a few months later.

Benjamin said he mentioned his grandfather as 'old Grossbaum' because he was head of a massive family of 11 living children and a number of grandchildren. He remembers his grandfather as an enormous photo–square frame, broad, off-white beard, round cap, serious expression on his face with a radical shine in his eyes. He remembers listening to various stories during his young years about his grandfather's supreme devoutness, so much so that he had his own *Beth Hamidrash* or Educational Hall, where scholars and devotees came to pray and study. However, much later his paternal uncles told some different stories regarding his grandfather. Benjamin's uncle told him about their oppressive upbringing by his grandfather at their house and about the restrictions that they had on all kinds of entertainment or against secular activities. They were even restricted from blowing whistles at home informed his uncle. Notwithstanding all his restrictions, the patriarch was only 56 at the time of his demise.

Benjamin remembers that his father had brought a newly invented phonograph from one of his journeys that he was showing to his siblings in a room on the ground floor of his grandfather's house. Unfortunately the record that he played had a sound of a whistle in it. His grandfather, who was in his study on the first floor, came out angrily shouting at the person whistling downstairs.

Benjamin's father replied smiling that no one was whistling and asked his father to come down and listen to his new phonograph. Remembering what his uncle Will told about the incident, Benjamin said that his grandfather returned to his study without uttering another word. After all he could not have gone against the economic base of the entire family.

Benjamin remembers having a phonograph at his 128th Street house. It was probably during the year 1900. Benjamin found the horn of the phonograph most impressive that was even bigger than him in size. He recalls that the records were on wax cylinders, similar to those that were later used for Dictaphones. Every record started with the announcement of its selection and name of the artist and with a kind of victory song 'Edison Recccords!'.

He recalls that his father was fond of accumulating things, particularly those that were new during those times and also that were unusual. He left behind three gold watches after his death. One of them was a 'repeater'—that is when you press a button, probably in the middle of the night—it would tell first the number of hours, then fourth of an hour, then the remaining minutes. He said after his father's death, his mother told them that each one of them would get one of these watches at the time of the initiation ceremony—*Bar Mitzvah*, at the age of 13 when they would assume all the duties and privileges of a full Jew. However, unfortunately this promise could not be fulfilled. After the death of his father, due to financial crises these watches were also either sold or put on mortgage with all the other valuable things never to be retrieved. Benjamin recalls about being benefited from only one item out of all that his father left behind—an English blazer coat, which somehow his mother successfully managed to save and keep for all those years. Benjamin remembers wearing this coat as part of his tennis attire when he played at the public court.

Wearing the coat, Benjamin realized that his father was a lean built man because the coat fitted him at the age of 18. However, being adversely commented on his attire by his friends, Benjamin finally gave up on his only inheritance.

He remembers that his father's health was deteriorating even before the death of his grandfather. He was getting pale and they were told that he suffered from a mysterious disease named 'yellow jaundice' or jaundice. However, with his sick father, they had made another shift in their residence and went to live in an apartment house 'The Ferncliff' that was at 120th Street and Seventh Avenue. It was universal moving day till the 1st of May. Remembering the apartment, Benjamin recalls that it must have been a cold afternoon in Spring because he saw his parents warming themselves in front of a wall of blue flame coming out of the chimney that he found was a new gas-based heating technique.

By this time, Benjamin was grown enough to be naughty at some level. At this time he was mainly under the influence of his second brother Victor, who was known for being a nuisance since childhood. Remembering one of their muses, Benjamin said towards the south of their house at Seventh Avenue, there were several shops selling flowers. There was one greenhouse behind these shops. Influenced by his brother Victor, Benjamin prepared a rope with several knots that was attached to a big screw. This screw was pulled out from the centre with a special kind of red rubber washer used in the beer bottles those days. All they had to do was smear the rubber pad with saliva to wet it wet and stick it on the glass wall of the greenhouse. It used to stick on the glass wall immediately through vacuum. Then they wrapped the knotted rope on their finger and every screw after the knot fell before the glass with a click making the sound of bullets being fired from a machinegun. Hearing the sound, the owner of the greenhouse ran after the culprits threatening them. Though all involved succeeded fleeing from the block by the time the owner came out.

Benjamin had a strong start of his school days after they shifted to Ferncliff. He was admitted to the primary section of

Public School 10 situated at the 117th Street, St. Nicolas Avenue. The school was still an old one as indicated by its lower digit; however it had a good reputation in scholarship and athletics. Benjamin remembers spending probably only one session or half-a-year in the primary section and started with grade 3A in September and was sent to grade 4A by next February. This was where they started teaching grammar. Benjamin found the Principal of the Primary section—Ms. Roberts, very ancient and divine. (Though, she was probably just 40 years at that time). They had assembly once a week and by making a simple arrangement of moving around the movable walls of the classes, they changed it into one big hall for the purpose. There was a stage in front where Ms. Roberts used to sit—sometimes with a guest. Benjamin remembers a quote written on the glass window behind the stage –

Honour and shame from no condition rise,
Act well your part; there all the honour lies.

– Alexander Pope

Benjamin joined the class of Ms. Churchil among the boys of the grammar department with pride on February 1, 1903, when he was not even nine years old. Ms. Churchil was fair, beautiful and was the centre of attraction of not only some male teachers of the school but some adolescent boys of her class, remembers Benjamin. These students readily agreed to stay back for hours for extra classes or to help in various jobs. He muses, this all took place in some other universe that was far from the thoughts and dreams of a young and short boy. However, Benjamin confesses being in love with Ms. Churchil because she was not only beautiful, but an affectionate person too.

Unfortunately Benjamin's family suffered a massive tragedy amidst this pleasant environment. His father's health suddenly deteriorated and had to be taken to a German hospital. He was operated for some unknown internal situation. It was much later that Benjamin found out that his father was operated for pancreatic cancer. It was towards the end of February when all three brothers were called out of their respective classes and were taken to the hospital by their governess. At the hospital they were told that they could see their father for a brief moment and that they had to be very quiet. It was since that day that the picture is ingrained in Benjamin's memory that he entered the room and saw his father wrapped in bandages. However, he says, clearly this description was nothing but an added memory. Although he believes that his father laid his frail hand on the head of all three boys and blessed them. He remembers kissing his father more out of love as a son and out of nervousness and then they all came out of the room.

He was then taken to his uncle Emanuel's house for their afternoon meal and their *Mademoiselle* kept giving them appropriate instructions while on the way, which he innocently considered to be true. That was the reason when Benjamin's 15 year cousin Ethel enthusiastically asked him about what was going to happen, he innocently, but bravely answered that his father was getting better. Strangely, she asked with half relief and half surprise that was he not dying? To which Benjamin replied, "absolutely not". However his brothers were silent. Then his 'bad' brother Victor, who was more open and emotional of the three, picked up a prayer book and started to read some Hebrew prayers with teary eyes.

Later they returned to their house and the wait began. Finally the door opened and someone brought their mother inside the house. She was crying miserably. Seeing the scared faces of her children, his mother declared, "My children, you are all orphans now". Benjamin remembers that they all started crying too as he would understand that things would be different from now on, painfully different. He remembers reliving those moments repeatedly in his dreams and always imagined that he rushed towards his mother and wrapped his arms around her and said, "no mother we are not orphans, you are still with us".

His father, Isaac M. Grossbaum, was buried at the Washington graveyard at Long Island, which was situated at a very distant place. He remembers following the hearth van in a four-wheeler. He remembers pouring some soil after the coffin was laid in the earth. He remembers making a stop for some food and hot beverage after leaving the graveyard because it was a very cold day. Benjamin says that it was inevitable that the memories of his father's death, which had almost vanished from his memory, were to re-emerge after quarter of a century. He says he was almost his father's age, and a father himself, when he realized it was his eight-year-old son who was saying goodbye to the world. His dear first-born Isaac Newton, who was named after his grandfather he never saw, was lying lifeless in the coffin and the grieving parents laying fists full of soil on his little grave.

How did the death of Benjamin's father have an impact on his very being? He recalls, it was definitely in a more devastating manner than he had realized. Psychologists would assure that he was deprived of a necessary component of security and normal upbringing and that the experience of his father's death made a deep painful impact on him. However, his clarity forces him to accept that in his self-discovery the results were not that bothering. It was probably that the constant absence of his father and lack of his cooperation with them lessened the impact of his death on his three sons. Benjamin adds that they do not miss their father because he was actually never with them.

It is a tribute to his mother's intelligent upbringing that they grew up like real boys – free of the threads of her apron and prepared to take on the manly responsibilities as soon as possible. Adversity is bitter, but its uses may be sweet. Their loss was huge, but in the end they could calculate the big compensation.

With the death of his father, a new chapter opened for the material life of Benjamin's family. This was a long and painful duration that began with a sort of downfall that took them to even more complicated situations. Their fight went on and continued for several years. Each and every bit of whatever their father had left behind was either gone or damaged over some troubled years. Even their mother's jewellery was put on mortgage never to be bought back. Fortunately, several of his mother's siblings were rich by that time who took care of Benjamin and his family during those troubled anxiety-ridden years.

Benjamin remembers that it was a massive downfall for his mother who was owner of a huge house a little while ago assisted with a cook, servant and a French governess, now had to live with her three sons on a meagre amount of 75 American dollars a month.

❑

In Public School

Benjamin's character was built up in the three years after the death of his father. Between the year 1903 and 1906, he lived at 244 West 116th Street and attended Public School 10. At the time of his admission, Benjamin was an innocent sensitive child. When he graduated, he had already realized that he had to stand strong against the adversity of fate, had to earn through various means and simultaneously concentrate on what he had to achieve. Above all, he realised that he had to rely on no one other than himself to understand himself, to encourage himself and for almost every other thing.

Was this change good for him in totality? Benjamin muses, probably it was. However, others have sharply disagreed with him. They say that the pressures and difficulties he faced during those initial years have affected his character. It raised a huge wall between him and the world around him because of which it became impossible for him to be friends with other people or have a permanent loving relationship with them. Benjamin says that he would discuss these negative possibilities later. At this point, he would only describe the process of adjustment of a young child with the world around him, which mainly appeared ruthless to him.

Considering the love and attention being given to the children these days, Benjamin finds himself comparatively deprived of all these things. However, the facts are opposite. He says, he got all sorts of support when needed; otherwise he was left on his own to be strong. Citing an example, Benjamin says, he went for ice-skating at the Central Park Lake right under the 110th Street on one very cold winter day. He remembers that he walked to the lake for skating and walked back home. He was freezing with cold and on the verge of crying due to pain. His mother helped him change his clothes, made him sit near the fire, rubbed his hands to make them warm and served him hot tea. One might say that this is natural and does not prove anything. However, in retrospect Benjamin finds that the incident left an everlasting impact on his mind because this was the only time—other than when he was sick and in bed—when his mother (or anyone else) had showed this kind of concern for him for such a small physical condition. He recalls that they treated their own wounds in their house unless they were too severe. They never complained about anything in the house.

His relations with his brother also strengthened him to a great extent. His brothers were not the type who would boss or dominate anyone; rather they had a special love towards Benjamin that continued for over 60 years. However they were older than him and were more strong and practical. He says that it was not expected from his brothers to be selfless or sweet during the initial stages of youth. Fortunately, he does not remember any particular example of being mistreated or treated in an unjust manner by them either, although, he remembers the feeling of being misused by his brothers. Benjamin once made a resolve with bitterness to inform them regarding their wrong doings. He planned to prepare a list of his brothers' harsh words and inappropriate deeds and write 'forgiven' on it and to give it to them as a birthday present. However, he chickened out later.

His massive family comprising members of Grassbaums and Gesundhits lived in a nine-room flat with just one bathroom. Benjamin believes that it must have taken some management, thoughts and many miracles to make that one bathroom sufficient for such a huge family. He, however, does not remember facing any difficulty or problem that might have emerged out of such a few resources. He remembers that they somehow managed to get the things they needed – that included not only food and clothes but also things like skates, baseball equipment and later tennis rackets and balls. Benjamin says unlike present days, the prices of items were very minimal during those days and that they only bought them at even cheaper rates.

He wonders from where they got the money to buy all these things? Benjamin assumes that they got some pocket money—probably 10 cents per week and a slightly larger amount on their birthdays. However, he recalls, apart from this, they tried to earn even the smallest of money from whatever small jobs they could grab or from whatever they invented. He says that like all other families they had also subscribed to *Saturday Evening Post*, the most popular weekly magazine of that time. The publisher of the *Post* used to put an advertisement for earning opportunity for boys to sell the *Post* on the streets and to advertise for getting the annual subscription of the *Post*. Benjamin remembers that he was only nine years old when he registered his name for the job. He received 30 copies per week of the *Post*. They sold it at 1 nickel per copy and paid 3 cents per copy to the publisher. Benjamin remembers receiving a nice cotton apron along with the first shipment of the magazine that had a pocket for keeping the change. He remembers that he stood at one exit of the elevated line at the 116th Street and 8th Avenue and used to call—'Take your *Saturday Evening Post*, fresh, only for 5 cents".

Recalling his school days, Benjamin said he had a couple of very close coeval friends at that time and that they played on the streets after school. His closest friend was Sydny Rogo who lived at 111th Street and was quite wealthy compared to them. Benjamin often visited his block and they along with some other friends played stoopball, street hockey or roller skates. He remembers that there was one game that they often played - Cat. Cat was a pointed piece of wood similar to a clothes pin. It was hit on the sharp end with another big stick and once Cat was in the air, it was again hit as hard as possible with the longer stick to be thrown far away. The opponent party used to try and catch it and if they failed to do so, they had to throw the Cat towards the large stick, used to hit the Cat at the first place, and was now lying on the ground. There was a scoring system based on the distance between the Cat thrown by the opponent player and the long stick that was used to hit the Cat.

Benjamin remembers that once during some game he scared his mother to death. Recalling the incident, Benjamin said that during some game he found himself standing in the centre of the main road with traffic moving from both the sides honking horns. He said he doesn't remember whether it was out of fear or helplessness but he somehow stood between the tracks on a thin road. The vehicles passed besides honking horns. Then he vanished from the sight—he recalls—right in front of his window from where unfortunately his mother was watching him with scared eyes. As soon as the vehicles separated, Benjamin said, he waved his hand towards his mother. His mother, however, was dumbfounded due to the whole episode. Benjamin recalls that he himself was not feeling very comfortable as he saw the vehicles getting too close to him on the road.

Though not a very mischievous child, Benjamin remembers that he had only one boxing fight of his life at the age of eleven years with Joseph Vermilyea who lived in a rented accommodation on the second floor across the landing. He was Benjamin's age and had an older sibling, a sister named Hazel, who was three years older than them. They were friendly, but not actual friends due to the difference in their religious beliefs. However, Benjamin does not remember the reason for the fight but remembers standing on the street in front of their house surrounded by his brothers and some other children who urged them to get into the fight. The fight did not last for more than two minutes with no one hitting the other. That so-called fight was broken by some adult leaving the two young ones relieved and the spectators disappointed.

Benjamin wonders how he managed to escape from other physical struggles in his later years as he was a quiet reserved person by nature and never started any fight. He however wonders why others ever abstained themselves from challenging him? He assumes that probably he had been quite a lucky person throughout his life. Another less possible definition, he assumes, could be that he used to hang-out mostly with the boys older than him during his adolescent years and it was against the junior chivalry to force a younger boy to fight. The third definition, he assumes, could be that he had something that protected him from the hostile acts of others. Almost everyone liked him in a watchful, protective manner. Apart from this, Benjamin felt that he was actually not one of the gang.

Recalling another friend, Benjamin said that he had a friend called Kaufman who was the son of a tailor. He used to put a couple of posters announcing the current or upcoming shows of the movies that were screened at theatres nearby. For this he used to get two free tickets. Benjamin recalled that Kaufman took him a couple of times to the matinee shows and those were the greatest incidents of his life. However, his friendship with the tailor's son was not welcomed by his family members. He said that though his family was unable to spend money on other things, however, they could always afford the luxury of class-conceit.

Then there was a mysterious boy who was Victor's friend, continues Benjamin, who used to visit their flat from time to time. This mysterious friend of his brother always had pockets full of money. As his memory recalls, Benjamin said, that boy used to sit on a bed or chair and threw a fist full of coins in the air spreading them in the entire room. He then shouted 'scramble' with kindness on his face. Then the three brothers got on their hands and knees in front of him collecting those pitiful coins that were so important to them, recalls Benjamin.

Apart from whatever was happening out of school, Benjamin said his main interest during those days was his studies. He was a good diligent student who was dedicated to gain education and also extremely ambitious to set an excellent academic record.

Remembering an important incident that took place at the New York City School when he was in his sixth year—'Maxwell Exams'. They were named after the Superintendent of the Schools, Dr. Maxwell, who announced that he was dissatisfied with the level of teaching and educational potential in the city. He personally prepared a series of exams for English and Mathematics that was to be given to all in the primary system. They were considered extremely difficult for their respective grades and were tested very rigorously. Benjamin said he was disappointed to know that he scored only 68 marks in English. However he later found them impressive when he found out that the student who ranked second had scored 42 marks.

It was the Mathematics exam that actually broke his heart, recalls Benjamin. He said he saw five questions on the blackboard in front of him that were apparently easy. He finished those questions early, submitted his answer sheet and walked out of the room. Later his principal, Dr. Birkins, called him to his office and asked why he had not answered the last two questions. "You can guess the story now", said Benjamin. He said question no. 6 and 7 were on the blackboard towards the back of the class that he completely missed. He even missed the announcement that the teacher made in the class regarding those two questions. He further added, though he had answered the first five questions correctly, he scored 70 marks that was the best record in the school. Recalling the disappointment of Dr. Birkins, Benjamin said his words were, "If you had answered those two questions as well, then you would have brought laurels to the school along with yourself".

Speaking about his school days, Benjamin said they became his most interesting days when he entered the "Departmental System" in Grade 7A in PS10. However the first day of that rank was not at all honourable for him. Soon after the commencement of office, Benjamin was suddenly promoted from 6B to 7A, and because this happened for the fourth time, Benjamin was hardly 10 years at that time when the Assistant Principal brought him to his new class along with some other boys. There were around 40 students, all boys, recalls Benjamin. He said those students looked towards him and laughed out loud. Amidst those Norfolk suit wearing boys of 12 years of age, Benjamin was the one still wearing the combination of sailor blouse and pants that indicated a young boy. Benjamin made a big scene at his house that afternoon about the outfit that his mother unwillingly took him to 125th Street and bought his first Norfolk suit.

Speaking about his first big income, Benjamin says that his talent for mathematics paved his way to earn some big bucks that time. He said one of his friends Chester Brown who was a grade ahead of him and much taller than him was performing badly in algebra. To improve upon his performance, Chester's mother called Benjamin to teach him algebra for which she paid 50 cents per week for three chapters. Recalling the time, Benjamin muses that he cannot comprehend the situation where he was teaching the subject that he had himself not studied by that time at school. Therefore, he said that there has to be something missing in the details of the story. He however remembers that he was taking tuitions at that time and continued it more or less till he had taught the sons of General Leonard Wood and other officers on the Governor's Island.

Benjamin added that his Public School career ended on a successful note. He had scored the highest average marks and surpassed his closest friend Sydney Rogo. This earned him the title of Valedictorian and earned him the right to become editor of the school magazine, *Wide Awake*. Although he felt proud delivering his valedictorian address at the graduation exercise, he does not remember if he did much other than writing a long poem. Benjamin was even more proud when after the address his favourite teacher Mr. Ben wrote the following words of respect in his green autograph album in beautiful handwriting that said,

To Poet, President and Valedictorian
With best wishes
– Stefan F. Ben

Speaking about his time at PS10, Benjamin said his days there ended in regret. Recalling the event, Benjamin said that the graduating class insisted on purchasing the School Pin that was made of solid gold costing 5 dollars. Coming from the family who struggled to meet their ends, Benjamin was not allowed to ask for such an amount. However, in order to save his face and unwilling to accept his poor financial condition before his classmates, Benjamin was forced to ask for this money from his mother and to corner her with his demand. However, Benjamin lost that pin in less than a month and was left with nothing but a lifelong regret for his lack of true character in the incident. Benjamin added that he consoled himself with the thought that his weakness and false pride must have made his mother sympathetic towards him as she herself had been a victim of the same feelings over the years. During those days, he added, every family wanted to project themselves wealthier than they actually were. For his family, it was even more important that they should not appear as poor as they actually were. His mother tried her level best not to talk too much and with regret about their former and now lost glory. However, there was so much left to remind her of her lost wealth that it was difficult for her to forget the past. Benjamin adds that their old family friends remained loyal to them and never left them. However, the difference between their financial status and those of their friends' was clearly visible in his mother's eyes.

Benjamin said that he and his brothers were immersed in that depressing atmosphere and it had a strong and unhealthy effect on at least one of them. He believes that his natural inclination was always far from the physical and intellectual and even the spiritual side of life. However, the difficult circumstances of his childhood affected him no less than his brothers. These circumstances made Benjamin very conscious and respectful towards money. He realized that the primary symbol of success in life lies in big earnings and big expenditures. Benjamin adds that it is only after several decades and many ups and downs that he had mastered the simplest and most important rule of material well-being. He says that the best financial strategy is - to live within one's own means.

❑

High School Days: Brooklyn and the Bronx

After Benjamin graduated from PS10, he was recommended for higher studies for admission to the High School division of Townsend Harris Hall of College of the City of New York. The duration of the course study they had here was of three years as compared to four years in other institutions. However, here it was expected from the students to cover the syllabus equivalent to those of others or probably even more than that within the three years' duration. The merits of admission and retention were very high compared to others. Recalling his first day at this school, Benjamin said he had an opportunity to meet another boy of his own age, Fredric F. Greenman. The two immediately became friends and their friendship lasted their lifetime. Another classmate was Mauri Gottschalk, who was destined to become the dean of that huge college where he had entered with such a humble and apprehensive gesture.

Benjamin says that he had forgotten most of his teachers from Townsend Harris Hall. However, there are still two of them that he remembers—one is Eduardo San Giovanni, one very terrifying Latin teacher, who actually taught Benjamin this complicated language. The second was one very quiet and distinctive looking geometry teacher who was categorically opposite to the aggressive San Giovanni. His name was Morris Raphael Cohen added Benjamin. He further adds that though Morris Raphael Cohen was of no importance to anyone at that time, but he was destined to shine in the history of Philosophy. He further adds that clearly teaching geometry was not his qualification.

Benjamin recalls Townsend Harris Hall had its own distinctive syllabus that warranted massive hard work, and in this syllabus they were required to include twelve books of plain and compact Geometry in one academic year. He recalls that Mr. Cohen had not prepared the plan of their assignment properly and as a result they were way behind completing their course by the beginning of June. Benjamin remembers that the entire class was rendered startled one day when Mr. Cohen declared that tomorrow they would start the tenth book.

Benjamin remembers meeting Mr. Cohen after seven years in different circumstances when he was a senior at the Columbia College having an interest in Philosophy and French along with other subjects. He adds that Prof. Raymond Botrox of Sorbonne was in their college to give lectures on the subject, "Is Mr. Henry Bergson a Pragmatist?" Benjamin said that Prof. Botrox started his lecture by saying "yes ladies and gentlemen he is definitely a Pragmatist" and ended his lecture with the same enthusiasm saying "therefore Mr. Bergson is not a Pragmatist".

Benjamin recalls that after the lecture he was in a dilemma for what to take out of it when he saw his former Geometry teacher. Benjamin went over to greet him who greeted him back very politely. Benjamin says that in response to his courtsey he asked him in a very arrogant manner that, "Hello Mr. Cohen, do you have any interest in Philosophy too?" In response to this, Mr. Morris Raphael Cohen smiled and said, "A little bit", and walked away. Benjamin remembers that the student standing next to him looked at him with surprise. "Idiot", the student said to him, recalls Benjamin. The student asked and further elaborated to Benjamin that does he not know that Morris Cohen has been universally accepted as the successor of William James. Benjamin recalls that he had no idea about this and says that this experience gave him a life lesson—to never show grace to anyone with pride.

Going back to what was happening in his family, Benjamin says that his mother decided to move out of their Uncle Morris's house and start their own boarding house when he was still in school. They took a brownstone house on rent at the 129th Street. However, Benjamin does not remember how they managed to decorate the house. He remembers that his mother was not a very good business person, so much so that they learned it much later that the house they had rented to make the boarding house was opposite a rented stable. As a result with soaring heat and rising stink, the loss of situation worsened more for their tenants as compared to them.

Due to financial situations at home, the 12-year-old ambitious Benjamin felt the need to find a profitable job. He remembers that there was a dairy shop near a sexton bearing the magical poster saying "needed a boy". He recalls that when he applied for the job, the sexton manager told him in a doubtful manner that he was not capable enough for this job. Benjamin said that he assured the manager that he was and that he could trust his enthusiasm and honesty. The law during those days permitted persons of any age to work for summer jobs for any amount of money. Therefore, he was hired at 2 dollars a week. He further adds that initially everything was fine. He used to push a delivery cart full of goods to various houses in the neighbourhood, then take the goods to the godown, and search for bells and speaking tubes of the customers to contact them. He used to pull the dumbwaiter full of goods upwards and then downwards for money. Sometimes he had to pull it up again to return the remaining money. He recalls that later the delivery car was given to someone else and he was made to carry a loaded basket. This was quite tiring for the young Benjamin particularly in the harsh heat during the beginning of August. He remembers that once he kept the basket down to wipe his face and to give some relief to his aching arms, when two young boys, playing stoopball nearby, called over his shoulder, "work you horse", when he picked up the basket again to move forward. This broke his heart and then later his brother Victor, who was stronger than him, took over his job and performed much better, recalls Benjamin.

Benjamin says that by the end of summer they vacated their 129th Street *redolence* house and shifted their business to 350 Manhattan near 114th Street to another brownstone house. It was at this place that Benjamin experienced *Love* for the first time. Till this time he had basically divided women in two categories (a) Mother and (b) an alien. He remembers that this offensive behaviour was due to the circumstances of his education. He had never studied in a co-ed school other than the two weeks he had during his kindergarten days.

Recalling the memories of the days of his pre-adolescent love at the age of 12, Benjamin said that the inspiration of his infatuation was a beautiful, talented and a lively girl, with whom he fell in love. The strange thing was that the girl liked him too even at that tender age. Constance Fleishman, the girl he was in love with, came to live in their boarding house with her mother so that they could be close to Bernard College. He said that there could be no one more kind towards a shy boy like him other than Constance who offered to teach him French. Benjamin said he honestly offered himself to be her student even though he had various other subjects to study. Not long after he had a textbook version of Prosper Merimi's Columba in his library, complete in glossary, notes and the following words in Constance's beautiful handwriting on the title page, "I love glazed chestnuts".

The two used to read French poems together. Benjamin remembers a poem by Victor Hugo—"*La tombe dit à la rose*", which she said was her favourite poem and asked Benjamin to memorize it. He remembers it clearly even today that he did it not only out of enthusiasm but also translated it in English. This marked the beginning of one of the transitions of Benjamin's intellectual life. Like several romantic and contemplative men, he had also written many poems of his own. However, he adds, his critical spirit tells him that they lacked the divine spark in his poems. Yet, translating the masterpieces of others, he had benefited from their inspirations. Works like these needs dedication and a specific skill, and Benjamin felt that he successfully did the job. He felt personal satisfaction in various translating works in Greek, Latin, French and German languages and particularly in translating a poem in French by A.A. Hausmann.

Benjamin was now 13 years of age and therefore was being duly trained for the *Bar Mitzvah* ceremony. Recalling the time, Benjamin says that all he can say about this is that he had disappointed his spiritual mentor by his stubborn refusal to deliver a speech of gratitude to parents and a sincere commitment to the glory and observance of Judaism. After hearing countless such speeches in the Synagogue on Sabbath mornings, he was struck by a violent protest against their drab likeness, their sentimentality and their apparent hypocrisy.

He had lost his faith in short order says Benjamin. He realized that the elaborate and archaic rituals which he had earlier accepted unquestioningly were the enemy of both thought and comfort. Whatever the real meaning and appeal of great affirmations of religious faith to a sensitive mind was, it was suffocated under the plethora of repetitive jargon. He said that Sunday school was a scourge and the synagogue became boring. As the years passed, he added, his grip on Jewish customs and traditions became more and more loose, until eventually they almost disappeared from his horizon.

However, it does not mean that he had lost all his interest in the religion, said Benjamin. On the contrary, he added, religion in general had long been one of the main objects of his inquiry and attention. The variety of religious revelations, beliefs, and experiences had provided him with an infinite number of subjects to study. The contrast between man's undeniable need for religion and the questionable character of his religions is astonishing. It is difficult to deny the existence of God in the universe; but it is equally difficult to accept any of the myriad and conflicting doctrinal ways in which God is said to have revealed Himself to man. So much so, Monotheism—Judaism's gift to the world—was doubtful to his sceptical mind, adds Benjamin. He said, the idea of one God is alluring in its splendid simplicity, but whether it matches the preoccupations of the unseen world is another question. Recalling 'A Pluralistic Universe' (1909) by William James that he read in his college days, Benjamin said he was struck by his frank speculations, as they matched the ideas that were sprouting in his own mind.

Furthering his ideas on religion, Benjamin said that as a curious citizen of the western world, he was quite attracted by the principles and history of Christianity. He said Lord Jesus became his hero quite early in his life in a very amusing manner. He said, most of the gifts that he received at his *Bar Mitzvah* were books and one of them was sent by a young Rabbi who was a close friend of their family. The title of the book was *A Prince of the House of David*. Benjamin said when he read the book a few months later he was surprised to see that it contained a series of fictional letters describing the life and martyrdom of Jesus. The Rabbi's gift didn't convert him to Christianity, but it did introduce him to a character that never ceased to charm and intrigue him.

Speaking about the philosophy of religion, Benjamin says it is surprising to consider the change in religious orientation of regions of the Western world in a single lifetime. The ease with which some people have given up faith, even interest in religion, seems astonishing compared to the control it once had over the thinking of the crowd. Benjamin says he had often said to young people that, "one must think a lot about God before he has the right not to believe in Him". He further says that, however, to people religion appears like the earth's gravitational field to astronauts. Those who have broken away from their family's doctrinal traditions manage to establish a way of life that completely disregards religion without difficulty. However, he further adds, to the millions who find God, heaven and hell supremely real and millions of others who never even think about these notions, it is strange to think of symbiosis on earth.

Talking about his Jewish religion, Benjamin says that he should tell about his standpoint on the Jewish religion clearly, though briefly. He says that he cannot live without thinking that it has been a great misfortune for Jews to be born as Jews as a whole. Fate would have been kind to them if they had allowed them to be born as Christians. Nevertheless, he adds, he can say with equal clarity in his case that his Jewish birth brought him only minor losses, which are largely compensated by some gifts of mind and personality bestowed upon him by Judaism.

Benjamin observes it appears that many Jews have a low opinion about the Jewish people - at least for those who were born in some less popular regions of the world. He says, however he was not one of them. Benjamin feels that where on one hand the Jewish character has been largely insulted, on the other hand, it has been raised to some level too. The Jewish character suffered humiliation and oppression for several centuries that had roughened it and also refined it. Benjamin shares one of his theories about it, which he feels is a curse to most of his Jewish friends. It says, the real mission of the Jews was to intermarry and thus contribute their hard-earned talents and abilities to a wider set of people. What a wonderful adventure it would be in genetics! adds Benjamin.

Speaking about his mother's adventure with business, he says his mother's career as a boarding house keeper ended in a destructive manner. A red flag was raised in front of their house and they lost almost all their assets in auction. Benjamin remembers swinging between the embarrassment of being humiliated publicly for being sold-out at the bang of a hammer and the excitement of the crowd, the activities and the oddities. He says that he along with his older brothers was given some work to do on the day of the auction. Since he was the mathematician of the family, he was made to add up the income received from the auction of furniture of each room. He remembers that his mother looked sad after everything was sold at a ridiculously low price. In the end, he remembers, his dear piano got two high bidders and that magnificent thing was sold to one of them for 150 dollars. He adds that for the entire day this was the only moment when he saw a little smile on his mother's face.

Benjamin recalls that after the auction they were left with no other option than to go and live with his Uncle Maurice at Barough Park. This place was considered far from the centre of things and particularly far from the Townsend Harris Hall at Amsterdam Heights in Manhattan. To commute to the Townsend Harris Hall he had to travel first through a street car followed by a BRT elevated train across Brooklyn Bridge and then the newly constructed Metro line for 137th Street Broadway, which amounted to almost one-and-a-half hours both ways. Benjamin recalls that time was not that much of an issue; however the most painful was the double fare of 1 dollar a week that he had to pay. He adds that amidst all this travelling, he had never wasted his long time spent in the trains. He used to finish almost all his homework while commuting to and fro to the college and home. He remembers studying Greek language while travelling through Brooklyn Bridge and looking up from his book in between to glance at the red dots under construction at Manhattan Bridge.

Talking about the financial status of his family, Benjamin remembers that being a 13-year-old boy he could manage to gather small amounts through every possible way. He remembers to even taking care of coal mine, teaching mathematics to a boy named Barrondes who lived in his neighbourhood. His father, Joseph Barrondes, was a famous Labour radical. Their families became friends and Benjamin found him fortunate enough to have witnessed various enthusiastic discussions between the two brilliant men—his Uncle Maurice and Barronades. He adds that the main source of his petty income came from typing the reports prepared by his Uncle for his various customers.

Speaking about his first ever earned possession, Benjamin said he added up the money he earned with what he received for his birthdays and bought himself a bicycle. He remembers that the day he bought this bicycle was the very important day of his life. He dragged the bicycle to a deserted road and learned how to ride it after many scrapes and bruises. He said the bicycle turned out to be a blessing during summer when he used to ride it along with his neighbour and friend Cloud Gasnor to an athletic league ground of a public school in Flatbush where they played tennis with enthusiastic confidence.

Going back to learning French, Benjamin says he made a serious effort to learn French and continued to build on the delicate foundation of his lessons with Constance. The only French book left in Grossbaum library was Bernardin De Saint-Pierre's '*Études de la nature*' recalls Benjamin. He adds, like any other book of the library, his father had bought this one too from the collection of Sir Moses Montefiore on sale. He remembers the book was once in a pristine condition, but now the binding seemed to be melting. The copy they had was printed in six small volumes of about 1800 pages. The pages were yellow, its print old and not very clear. In fact the French itself appeared to be ancient. Saint-Pierre was a distinguished French writer of the eighteenth century—a naturalist, a future general scientist and a romancer—all in one. He wrote extensively about plants and animals and his various scientific theories, one of which was that the tides were caused by the melting of ice at the poles!

Benjamin remembers referring each and every word of the book whose meaning was unknown or indefinite for him in the French dictionary by Heath and used to write it on a paper along with its English counterpart. He then hid the English and French parts of those lists and tried to do appropriate translations in both languages. By the end of the summer he had acquired an additional, albeit special, vocabulary of a thousand words. Later, he sometimes surprised his French professors by using overly specific or archaic words in his conversational efforts.

At one point his Uncle Maurice became wealthier and moved to a lavish apartment in Washington Heights and they moved further in Brooklyn to a small place called Bath Beach Section. He remembers his mother was once again happy to be independent and all of them embraced the limitations of their modest flat in the best of spirits.

Benjamin recalls that it became more difficult for him to continue studying at the Townsend Harris Hall owing to increased distance from his place of residence and hence with much reluctance he had decided to enrol in Boys High School in Brooklyn, which had a standard four-year curriculum. With childish pride, Benjamin had made up his mind to enter college at the glorious age of fifteen, and changing high school meant giving up that futile ambition.

Recalling his days at the Boys High School, Benjamin says a new Headmaster Dr. Sullivan had joined the school that year who later went on to become a historian of New York state. When Benjamin went to see him in his office with his Townsend Hall report card, he first welcomed Benjamin in an ordinary manner. However, after going through his report card, Dr. Sullivan's round face turned into a huge smile. With this smile on his face, Dr. Sullivan told Benjamin that "This is the type of report card that he would love to see". He told Benjamin that "Most of the boys who come to me from Townsend Hall are those who were thrown out of there because they failed to achieve the desired grades and I was forced to accept them. Though they only reduced our average". It was then Benjamin realized that in fact Boys High School long had the highest reputation for academic excellence in the country and that he was really fortunate to be admitted there.

Benjamin spent two fruitful years in the Boys High School. Though due to scheduling difficulties he was unable to continue with his Greek. However, he devoted himself to Latin courses with particular enthusiasm. Benjamin says that classical languages have given immense value to his inner life. Nevertheless, he does not support the compulsory study of Latin and Greek, nor does he place as much emphasis on these subjects as to learn them willingly. These two languages are expensive mental luxuries, paid for by hours of hard work. Diligence in itself is not a bad thing; however, he sees it as a tragedy because the time and effort put in by so many of his fellow students practically ended up in vain. Benjamin adds that even he had forgotten every thought and almost every word after a few years.

He remembers that his achievements at the Boys High School were generally very impressive. He scored third position in his class and also contributed to his school's annual literary publication, *The Recorder*, with a story "The Great Pai-Plot". He also participated in some inter-class debates. However the greatest of his achievements was his election in Arista, a society of honour to all High Schools in New York, founded in his graduation year. Yet, the event that gave him the most satisfaction was winning the school tennis tournament. Since he was considered a studious student at Boys High School and possibly equally useless in athletics, his tennis victory would have greatly enhanced his reputation amongst his classmates, only if the timing had been correct. Since the tournament he participated in ended after his graduation, virtually no one even heard the world-shaking news of his success. In fact, he even received his medal the next fall by their athletic director who surprisingly asked him, "How did you do that"?

It was after this that they again shifted their place of residence and went on to live from Brooklyn to Kelly Street in the Bronx.

Nurturing the inventive side of his brain, it was at the age of fifteen that Benjamin thought of an invention—one of the many inventions that often struck his brain in his life. The visitor visiting people living in flats, as theirs', used to ring the bell downstairs, which further rang another bell in the kitchen. Then someone from the house pressed a button that unlocked the latch to the main gate downstairs granting admission to the visitor in the building. And because he was the youngest in the family, he was the one who pressed the button to unlock the main gate even when he was studying. It was his annoyance from this job that became the mother of his invention. Recalling his invention, Benjamin said he calculated that he could run some wires from bell to the button so that the motion of the bell ringer would close a circuit and open the bottom latch. He was successful in preparing the device after several attempts that finally worked. He had also put a small switch in the wiring so that the gadget could be turned off when they all went out and did not need to open the door. Its working was simple, as soon as someone rang their bell, the latch would start rattling and the visitor could open the door. Meanwhile, because of the sound of the bell, they were alerted about the visitor. Enthralled by his invention, Benjamin started dreaming of his invention being installed in every flat all over the world. The cost would be very low and it could easily pay them 1 dollar for every installation and could be (initially) installed by the owner. Then, of course he would get huge royalties from the licensees in other cities. The impractical dreamer of the family was going to restore their fortunes. In fact, it was taking him to the new heights of prosperity.

However, his triumph was only short-lived as Benjamin recalls that his dream soon crashed before him. What was the problem? First and foremost was the technical issue. The latch only rattled as long as the visitor put his finger on the bell. For example, explains Benjamin, a visitor would ring the bell and his attention was immediately drawn to the rattling of the latch. He would remove his finger from the bell to hold the door latch. Unfortunately, as soon as his finger was removed from the bell, the sound would immediately stop and the door would get locked again. The disappointed visitor would repeat the procedure, perhaps several times, always with the same result. By that time one of the family members would come to their rescue from the house, adds Benjamin. He said following this they would give a weak explanation inviting the visitor's comment that he didn't like their invention. But worse than those who did not know how to operate their gadget were the few who understood how to operate the gadget. Like for the children of the apartment it did not take too long for them to understand its operation. They would ring the bell fearlessly and open the door by putting their other hand on the knob and then enter the apartment and run to their respective flats. Whereas, Benjamin and his family were kept wondering about the whereabouts of their guests. He said soon all this became beyond his mother's tolerance and she ordered him to throw away this worthless thing, which he did with an aching heart. Not one to give up on challenges, Benjamin kept considering various ways to solve this problem, but actually didn't do anything about it.

❑

Farmhand and Mechanic

It is 3:30 in the morning in June 1910. The Erie Railroad terminal in New Jersey City looks like a giant, empty barn; only a half-eye of darkness could pierce the outline of the waiting room where he was sitting. There is a dot of yellow light in one corner that is coming from a telephone booth with the door half open.

The only resident of the narrow booth of that sprawling building was a recently turned sixteen-year-old teenager. This boy was none other than Benjamin Graham. He was sitting in an uncomfortable position leaning on the small seat near the equipment. Under a green light attached to a wooden shelf, he held a heavy green bind book. It was the forty-fourth volume of Francis Bacon, Baron Verulam's *Library of Universal Literature: The Magna Instauratio*, "The Advancement of Learning".

This was no adventure that Benjamin would feel proud about. It was a misunderstanding combined with some misfortune.

Remembering his stupid mistake that happened a day before, Benjamin was imprecating himself for being shy in such a childish manner.

Benjamin had left his house the day before after lunch and saying goodbye to his mother. He was leaving for New Milford, New York to work as the summer hired hand at Mr. Jacob Barman's farm as a junior grade. This arrangement was made by the mathematics professor of his Boys High School Dr. Weaver. Under his cap and sharp style, Dr. Weaver was known for his complete dedication to help city boys to experience the healthy discipline of life and labour in the countryside. Benjamin got easily convinced by his eloquence and along with three other boys submitted his name for the summer apprenticeship on a farm. The salary offered was 10 dollars per month with accommodation.

It was for the first time that Benjamin was leaving his mother to travel afar after he lost his father seven years ago. Clearly his mother got emotional at the time of his leaving. However even with teary eyes she bravely uttered that inevitable aphorism, "Take care son and write to me". Benjamin hurried down the stairs carrying his mother's black suitcase and almost immediately felt like a mature man. He was carrying a ticket to New Milford sent by farmer Barman and about 5 dollars in cash.

He reached Erie terminal an hour early by travelling via metro till Cortland Street and then through a ferry till New Jersey. Recalling the incident, Benjamin said he sat down on one very uncomfortable long bench and took out Bacon's book from his bag. He had packed several books for his journey. However they were strictly for formal studying—Anabasis in Greek and a standard Greek grammar—by Greenaf and Kitrez that he had received as a gift from the head of Classical Languages Dr. Rees of Boys High School. He also remembers carrying a red paperback volume with heading—"The Palmar Method for Perfect Penmanship". This book was also a gift to him by another teacher—not as an appreciation for his graphic skills but to improve one of his weaknesses. He had a very bad handwriting which his family graciously claimed that this flaw in Benjamin was proof that he was a genius. However, Mr. Edwards of his English department had a different opinion and had deducted

5 marks from work for bad handwriting saying, “It does little to make up for the damage done to my sight and disposition”. Hence, Edwards, in a genuine gesture, gave Benjamin palmer exercises, ceasing a promise from him that he would honestly practise his handwriting over the long summer evenings.

Out of all Bacon’s works there was only one book left in Benjamin’s family’s almost wiped-out library that he had not read even once. Sitting in the waiting room of the Erie Railroad terminal Benjamin was turning the pages of Bacon’s book slightly before the train was to arrive. When it was almost time for the train he went over to the ticket window and asked the man sitting inside about the track on which the train to New Milford was about to arrive. The man replied with crude voice that it was expected on track 9 at 5:12. Benjamin was surprised by the reply because the ticket he received from farmer Barman said that the train was scheduled for 4:30. However, Benjamin’s reluctance filled with shyness stopped him to counter the information and he went back to the waiting room and decided to read for some more time.

Still sceptical about the timings, Benjamin thought that the man at the window could be wrong about the timings and it was almost 4:30. He immediately stood and went back to the man at the window to inquire again. It was then that both the man at the window and he realised their mistake. The train Benjamin asked for was only ‘New Milford’ and the man at the window gave him the timings of the train to New Milford, Pennsylvania, whereas the train to New Milford, New York was rightly scheduled for 4:30 and the time left was only 10 seconds.

Recalling the biggest blunder of the day, Benjamin said he ran to catch the train. However, the doors shut right on his face and he missed the train because of his foolishness. The next train was scheduled for 5 the next morning. And now there was nothing that he could have done other than to wait for the next train which was about 13 hours of waiting. He was weighing his options and thought of going back home. However, his pride did not allow him to do so as he was not prepared to accept his mistake before his mother and could not face his brothers mocking him.

He decided it would be advisable to better wait alone and spent one hour roaming around in the Erie ferry at Hudson where he could ride the boat for an indefinite amount of time while on the boat. After having a cheap dinner and long stroll he came back to the station and had a small nap. In the end he went back to his bench with Bacon and started waiting for the train next morning.

Benjamin said it was his first time to be awake for so long and that he was too tired and sleepy. His body ached because of unnecessary strolling and waiting and everything dragged him towards sleep. However, he had to be awake with all his will power because he could not have afforded to miss the next train too.

Benjamin said with all that time on his hands he thought about himself—his recent graduation at the High School, his expectations from the college and his plans. Though his stupidity came returning back to his mind and he thought—"How can one man be that stupid?" It was not as if he was not satisfied with his achievements being a born student and a meritorious student throughout. However, his ambition was definitely to go to the college—preferably to Columbia and he had high hopes of winning one of the twelve Pulitzer scholarships—those splendid prizes that paid for the entire cost of studying and living away from home. It was for this purpose that he took part in the notoriously difficult college entrance board exams. After comparing his notes with a few friends and rivals, he was very sure that he would rank high on the list above hundreds of other candidates.

Benjamin said that amidst all that chaos he had so many reasons to be happy. He said that the poverty only grazed him after the death of his father. His father had nurtured his character with a serious concern for money, a willingness to work hard for even a small sum of money and a habit of extreme conservatism in spending it.

Remembering his time at the terminal, Benjamin recalled another obstacle that he had to face at 2 am that morning when all the lights at the waiting room went off and he was left all alone in darkness. It was probably because there was no other train scheduled till morning and that there wasn't any need to spend electricity on a vacant building, he added. With all the fatigue he was feeling, Benjamin fought with the will to keep up. He kept walking from one wall to another in the waiting room when he saw the only telephone booth besides the waiting room. He saw a small electric light in the cubicle that was working. Finding a relief, he went inside and kept his book on a small shelf and engaged in the twin task of assimilating Bacon's grand outline of a new world of knowledge and keeping his sleepy eyes wide open.

A little while later when Benjamin raised his eyes from the book he saw a ray of light in the earlier dark waiting room and realised that another long summer day was about to knock at the windows of the waiting room. He saw some other passengers entering the waiting room and felt relief that he was not alone anymore. He was confident that this time he would catch his train.

Recalling his time at farmer Barman's farm, Benjamin said he spent two months in his fields as a labourer which was one-fourth part of his 1 per cent life (1958) till that time. Nevertheless, he said, this short stay brought him more memories than many one year experiences. He said it was not that he was very happy in New Milford because he found the job daunting and boring and he looked forward to the day of liberation very impatiently, nor did he have any desire to go to the farm ever again, even as a non-labourer owner. Yet, it was not the suffering that craved so many visuals on his memory because he had never been abused at all, and anyway, he further adds, he had already acquired the ability to disregard the misdeeds of others. In fact, it was a complete change in the way he lived, especially at that impressive age, which explains the intensity and persistence of these memories.

Talking about the farmer, Benjamin said Mr. Barman was a 63-year-old man though he looked very ancient with his white beard and wrinkled face. He came to America from Germany with his parents after the political unrest of 1848. He joined the Union Army at the age of 18 when the civil war was towards its end. Remembering the old man, Benjamin said he doesn't remember whether or not Mr. Barman had ever fought in any war, but he was a complete soldier receiving a monthly pension which was the good source of his income. Mr. Barman had a small farm; a few acres around his farmhouse and a grass field at some distance from the road. He had two cows and both were named Lucy. He had some pigs and several chickens and an inevitable horse named Charlie that was used for both farming and for transportation. He grew various types of vegetables, fruits and grass for his livestock and alfalfa. He sold some milk from his cows and kept the rest for his own use.

The members of the Barman family comprised Mr. Barman, his second wife and a daughter from his first wife who was a teacher. Speaking about the Barman household, Benjamin said that the Barman women were casual with him; however they didn't get along with each other at all. One Mr. Snedekar used to join then during their meals, who ran the grocery store in the village. Sometimes some other men doing special work in the village were also present at the time of the meals. They used to pay handsomely for food to the Barman family. Their appetites were very good. Talking about their food intake, Benjamin said he still remembers one of them looking at him contemptuously while he was eating saying, "You call this eating eggs? I wouldn't dirty my plate with less than a dozen eggs".

Further talking about the Barman household, Benjamin said there was also an authentic secret in the house—an invisible resident. He was not to know about the secret about who that secret resident was for a very long time. However, after a few days of his arrival he came to know that everyone avoided going to a part of the house where someone was living.

Benjamin remembers that farmer Barman provided him with a small room containing a bed, almirah, a washstand and a kerosene lamp. There was no electricity or running water there and needless to say that there was no automobile or telephone in his house. The main source of water for household use was pumped from a well in the field, which usually was Benjamin's job. For bathing the water was heated in a kettle over a coal stove which was than mixed with cold water in a cloth tub which then Benjamin used to carry to his room to take a bath.

The work days there were long recalls Benjamin. He said Mrs. Barman woke him up at 5:30 in the morning and then he got ready immediately with sleepy eyes for his first job of the day—milking Lucy Senior and Lucy Junior. This was followed by loaded breakfast and then it was Benjamin's turn to feed the chickens and pigs and put the saddle on the horse and finish his other tasks allotted to him for the day. His day ended with another round of milking cows and feeding the chickens and pigs. Even Saturdays were the same as any other day. However on Sundays, he was allotted only holiday jobs. Benjamin said he used to work for 60 to 65 hours every week.

Benjamin said he had learnt a lot working in that farm and said it is a very difficult job to milk a cow. He recalls that his fingers got too tired before milking 12 quarters of milk from one cow and if one was not careful then the cow could cleverly tip the milk bucket. He said even the horse needed good care. It is particularly difficult to saddle the horse. It needs to be fed on a regular basis and similarly the cowshed needed to be cleaned from time to time. And then there were chickens and pigs too!

Benjamin found this job strangely distasteful. In his self-pity he compared himself to Hercules, who had worked for King Augeas; but for Benjamin there was no flowing river to help.

A proud student of farming, Barman was the only farmer growing alfalfa, comparatively unknown prior to that time. Barman described alfalfa as amazing that increases the amount of nitrogen in the soil and that the animals love to eat it. Unfortunately, to grow Alfalfa for its best result, it had to be grown on a hill and therefore the farmer had selected his steepest slope for the purpose. It was time to harvest. Benjamin remembers that they had used the grass mower to harvest Alfalfa and the machine had the natural tendency to slip down the slope. This is where Benjamin had his role. He said Barman sat comfortably behind the machine and he had to walk down the slopes in the scorching sun and push the machine in the opposite direction with all his might to prevent it from slipping down the slope.

Benjamin said cutting grass from a large pasture was less punishable compared to this. He had to stand on the hay cart to keep the bundles of hay being thrown in his direction by Barman as evenly as possible. It was pleasant to take a fifteen-minute break in the morning and afternoon to drink cold water from a small milk container placed in the shade of the leafy tree. At the end of the day it was even more pleasant to go home munching a straw over the hay cart. However, followed by all this, another not so pleasant task waited for him, which is known as 'cut the grass'. The farmer's entire harvest was stored in an attic built into the barn. This time the farmer would stand on the wagon and Benjamin stood at the little entrance to the haystack. As soon as the grass was thrown at him, he would hold it in his hands and take it to a suitable place in the cell. The grass was extremely hot and full of stifling dust. To Benjamin it seemed as though the work would never end; however it ended and then he was very happy to have finished the work.

Talking about another experience at the farm, Benjamin said that the farm is the best place for a young man to learn about sex. There is no such thing as innocence when you live among the animals on the farm, adds Benjamin. He said one day Lucy senior went in 'heat' and it was time to take her to a bull. A day was fixed for availing the services of a neighbour's animal. However, Mr. Barman had to go to a local fair and therefore the task was assigned to Benjamin, which proved to be a very difficult task for him.

Further recalling his days at the farm, Benjamin said after dinner and finishing all the day's work, he would go to his bedroom with a lamp and get ready to work on the self-direction. He studied Anabasis there with the help of Greek grammar. However, he added, he never read it in full, though finished a fairly large part of it. Thinking about the book, Benjamin said it never aroused his enthusiasm as a work of literature though he knew it was considered as a classic work.

Benjamin remembers meeting a few boys of his age in New Milford and that he spent some time with them. He remembers a particularly funny incident when one day he was describing the wonders of New York City while walking alongside the road and was boasting about various automobiles there that no one paid attention to anymore. Suddenly they saw a motorcar on the road that was approaching them at a very high speed. His friends immediately ran inside the adjoining field; however Benjamin kept walking carelessly besides the road. The motorcar honked wildly and drove off very near him. The driver must have thought that he might be crazy—which he was; however his friends were very impressed by his show of bravado.

While talking about the farmer's plantation, Benjamin said Barman's apple trees produced excellent fruits and he got the biggest and lustrous red apple he has ever seen in his life. He decided to send it to his mother. He wrapped the apple in paper and wrote the address on it and took it to the post office that was in a corner inside the general store. Mr. Snedekar, who was also the postmaster asked him how he wanted to send it? Benjamin replied he did not know and asked Mr. Snedekar the best way to send it and told him that it was an apple. "Apple!" surprised by the package, Mr. Snedekar might have thought these city people were definitely crazy, felt Benjamin. He added, Mr. Snedekar said that if he had to send it then he would have to send it through first class else it would rot and that Benjamin had to pay five times the cost to send it that way.

Benjamin felt that his intelligence, his devotion towards his family and his generosity—everything was being challenged. Nevertheless he decided to send it through first class. Those 89 cents that he had spent to send the apple was his petty treasure. His mother wrote to him that she appreciated his loving thoughts; however, it was unwise on his part to spend that amount of money on postage because the apple she received arrived in some suspicious condition.

Benjamin recalls that after some time his mother came to visit him at the farm. She almost always used to take a short summer vacation and this time she came up with a brilliant idea of staying at Barman's residence as a paying guest for a week, adds Benjamin. He said the farmer's family was happy to have her and receive another 8 dollars from her. She arrived in early August and it was a pleasant reunion for both Benjamin and his mother. His mother soon became friends with the three Barmans and within a few days she learned more about the farmer's family than Benjamin had known in a span of one month. In fact, adds Benjamin, it was she who solved the mystery of the secluded part of the Barman's house that was actually occupied by Barman's epileptic sister.

Benjamin said one day he received a letter from his brother Victor that was in verses. The letter had exciting information about the results of the Pulitzer Scholarship. It was like—"Hooray, Hooray! You won! You're seventh on the list!"

Benjamin said approximately twenty scholarships were to be awarded to contestants from all public schools in Greater

New York. He added that he would have felt really thrilled if he was ranked first, second or third. However, everyone assured him that there was nothing to worry about because he would be selected. The people from Pulitzer duly came to his house and his mother had a congenial interview with them. Following this interview a day was fixed for Benjamin's interview soon after his return to New York.

Finally it was 28th August, remembers Benjamin, when he said a friendly farewell to the Barman's family. This time he did not miss the train home. The old farmer himself came to see him off at the station.

As soon as Benjamin returned to New York, he went to World Building at Park Place for his interview for the Pulitzer Scholarship. The famous Chief Editor of the Pulitzer Daily Newspapers Mr. Alfred Harmsworth was his interviewer who was also the Chairman of the Scholarship Committee established under the inheritance of the great newspaper. Although, Benjamin was feeling very nervous, he was soon made comfortable by Mr. H and Benjamin found himself talking about his interests and aspirations with great enthusiasm.

Benjamin perceived that the interview went well. However when he discussed the interview with his family, he could hardly stop himself from being sure of the result.

Benjamin called the secretary to Mr. H after a week from the date of the interview as he was asked to do and was shocked with the response. "Please excuse me, but you are not selected" was the professional response of Mr. H's secretary.

Benjamin found himself dumbfounded for a few seconds and then asked in a weak voice, "Can you tell me whether Fred Greenman has been granted the scholarship or not?" "Greenman?" the voice asked, and replied, "Yes he has been granted the scholarship".

Benjamin recalled it was worse than the disappointment of not getting the scholarship. It was like a devastating blow for him. It was like all the hope and light had been drained out of Benjamin's life. It was not like that today Pulitzer Scholarship would appear to be very generous to him; however they used to pay 150 dollars per year to every winner of the scholarship to cover their college tuition fee for four years. And, apart from it if the receiver had to go away from his home to study, they were provided with additional 250 dollars a year to cover their expenses.

Recalling his mother's emotions, Benjamin said she was unable to bear the thought of her son being away for so long, and though he had a mighty yearning to follow Fred Greenman, who without hesitation had chosen the arrogant Harvard. Benjamin dutifully agreed to go to Columbia where he could commute while living at home. However, now all his plans were shattered. Neither Harvard nor Columbia was going to be the part of his dreams.

Benjamin remembers that his brother and his mother were equally upset about the unfortunate turn of events as he was; rather they were angry about it. They could not understand how those people could leave their "Benny" who ranked seventh in the list; whereas several of his friends along with those who were much below him in the list were selected. Benjamin said it might sound strange, but his mother blamed for everything on the furniture. He remembers even after removing most of the things from the house they still kept some of the chairs and sofas from Louis XVI and some other exquisite items. In spite of being in a dilapidated condition, the furniture still shed the slight aura of luxury. Pulitzer scholarships were awarded on the basis of need as well as academic excellence and good character. According to his mother the investigator must have concluded that despite their claim to poverty, he could actually afford to pay for college without a scholarship.

Benjamin had his own perception about his rejection. He felt that the reason for his rejection was the weakness of his character.

Benjamin said at that time he was struggling against a few things for years that the French called "*Mauvaises Habitudes*", which made a huge moral and physical issue by the combination of his innate puritanism and the dreaded health cults prevalent in those days. Benjamin told himself that the perspicacious Mr. H would have discovered this hidden distortion in his soul and awarded his scholarship to a purer and better person than him. After desperately wrestling with his problem, Benjamin added, he found himself reflecting on the strength of character of Abraham Lincoln, whose birthday they were celebrating on February 12, 1911. Benjamin decided that he would take Lincoln as his motivating force and would sought his help in maintaining the new and inflexible resolve that he imbibed that day. The idea worked for him and he realised that his bad habits ended.

Benjamin said even his mother soon recovered from this setback and returned to her serious and practical mode. He realised that if he could not go to Columbia then he had to go to the "College of the City of New York" where fortunately there was no tuition fee. Benjamin thought he could easily manage a part-time job to earn his pocket money in the city. He then duly took admission in the city college, though with a heavy heart, mainly because of his pure and unadulterated conceit. He added that though City College did not have professors like Harvard, Yale or Columbia, yet they had a good and strict curriculum that ensured well-trained graduates. The college alumnae consisted of various reputed people. Yet being a college with no tuition fee, most of its students hailed from the poor and lower class of society, who were generally uncultured or unsophisticated. And apart from all that, they were mainly Jews. For him going to the City College instead of Columbia was accepting inferiority and failure. Benjamin said looking at the matter as impartially as possible; he had to admit that there was some practical justification for this unreasonable conclusion. An attitude that reflected the general arrogance of America during 1911 was that a CCNY boy would be at some disadvantage in his professional and social career as compared to a graduate from a reputed college. His own acceptance of these distorted values intensified his sense of humiliation.

Benjamin was not happy at the CCNY as everything was inappropriate and unsatisfactory about the place in his sick state. He remembered that one day he left his college locker unlocked and later found two of his books missing. He felt very wistful and hopeless as he had to pay for those books and he had no source of pocket money. Out of this hopelessness Benjamin took an extreme decision that he would quit college and get a job.

Benjamin thought back about his earlier experiment and decided that the first thing he had to do was to collect parts of push button for the electric doorbell. Remembering the time Benjamin said that around six boys were standing around a table where various parts were lying in different baskets. After some directions, he learned how to fix those parts and became a complete part of the group. They used to work from 7 am in the morning till 5:30 pm in the evening with a 45-minute lunch break in between. Benjamin remembers that he possibly used to give 55 hours per week to the job, and adds that he never wanted to even calculate the hours he might have repeated the same job in a week.

Benjamin remembers that he recited poems to himself to spend the time. Fortunately he had a huge collection of them including the complete Rubaiyat of Gray's 'Elegy' and the first 400 lines of Aeneid. He used to sit aloof in the imaginary company of legendary poets; while his fingers were busy in their comparatively simple task moving efficiently, he added.

Benjamin in no time got fed up with the monotony of those push buttons and started looking at the 'Boy Wanted' segment of the *Sunday Times* again. One ad featured a job offer at a telephone machine shop a little far at 95 Fulton Street in Downtown, New York. The reason why the ad attracted Benjamin's attention was because they offered 5 dollars a week. He reached the small telephone shop very early on that Monday morning and saw a massive crowd of candidates. Soon the boss, Mr. L.J. Löffleir appeared and started taking interviews. He asked Benjamin about his education and was impressed to know that he was a High School graduate. Then he asked him about his experience, particularly about operating drill press. Benjamin replied that he knew how to operate drill press and got the job. He was to start from the very next day. Timings were from 7:30 am in the morning till 6 pm in the evening.

Four other boys got the job apart from Benjamin that filled the entire telephone shop. It was clear that not all of them were to be employed in the long run as was cleared by one of the three workers already working there. It was the annual plan of the old owner. Benjamin realised that the owner planned to prepare a big stock and most of them had the job till the work for the stock was over.

The telephone company of L.J. Löffleir had occupied only one floor in a small building. However, the shop was filled with lots of machinery and they manufactured in extraordinary amounts. The final product of the company was the telephone system for private consumers. Most of them were installed in the huge apartment houses constructed at Park Avenue, Fifth Avenue, West End Avenue and Riverside Drive.

For years after his apprenticeship, when Benjamin visited friends who lived along those streets, he would often look at the Löffleir nameplate on the switch board and wondered if his hands had helped in connecting those devices as well.

As promised to his mother, Benjamin wrote to Columbia in winter asking if he could apply for the scholarship to start in February. He received their reply saying that they did not offer any scholarship in the middle of the session. However, he could write again in the spring for the year starting September 1911. He did this in early April. Within days he received a strange note from Frederick F. Keppel, Dean of Columbia College saying that the scholarship he wanted to apply for was not available. However, the note further said, the Dean would like to discuss another matter with Benjamin at some convenient time and asked if he could make an appointment for the purpose with his secretary? Benjamin explained to them over the phone that he worked till 6 pm every day; however, he might be able to arrange to leave an hour early one day. He was told that in that case Dean Frederick F. Keppel would like to meet him at his house before 6 pm the next day. Hearing the response, Benjamin wondered what this could mean.

The next afternoon Benjamin washed his dirty hands with grease solvent as much as possible, took the Westside Metro from Fulton Street to 116th Street and walked the rest of the distance to the Dean's residence which was not that far. Recalling the day, Benjamin said he rang the bell with a throbbing heart. The door was opened by Mrs. Keppel who took him upstairs to the study where some firewood was burning in the fireplace. She said that the Dean would be with him in a while.

Remembering about the Dean and the encounter, Benjamin said within minutes the Dean entered the room. A tall, charming, elegantly dressed man whose practical gesture was combined with a charming smile. Then the tea arrived for them. Benjamin said he was conscious of the dirty work clothes he was wearing and the dirt residue around his nails. Dean Keppel talked pleasantly about his work for a few minutes while sipping the tea. And then, he turned to business.

Remembering the shocking conversation that took place with the Dean, Benjamin said the Dean started, "You know everyone in the registrar's office is very embarrassed about you and I share this embarrassment because I was a registrar at the university before I became Dean and I put in the system that went faulty".

Benjamin said hearing this he found himself in no position to comment.

The Dean continued, he added, "The thing is, Grossbaum, you got the scholarship here last year, but we didn't give it to you".

"How? How did this happen?" blurted Benjamin.

The Dean continued, "You have a brother or cousin Louis Grossbaum, who has been here on a Pulitzer Scholarship for the past three years. When we gave your award, the registrar's office messed up the names. They could not give a scholarship to the boy who already had one. So he gave the scholarship to the boy next to you in the queue".

Benjamin added, the Dean further told him that the award that he had won was the Columbia Alumni Scholarship, which provided full tuition and was awarded annually to the candidates with the highest average grade in the college entrance board exams. The Dean said he did this and added if he still wanted to come to Columbia College they could arrange to give him an Alumni Scholarship early next year. It would be just as financially good as the Pulitzer Scholarship of his late dreams, thought Benjamin.

However, he could only say, "This is interesting", then he calculated and said, "I have lost an entire year".

Dean Keppel said "This is true, and we are actually very sorry about this mistake". He asked Benjamin his age.

Benjamin said he was going to be 17 soon.

On this Dean Keppel said that it was very good and how he was not at all sorry. He said, "If you had started college a year early then you would have been too young to have gained benefits out of the college studies. Your machine shop apprenticeship is good for you. You would have more patience and maturity compared to other boys your age. As such, if you work hard you would get your degree probably within three years".

The interview ended on a sanguine note and Benjamin returned home full of enthusiasm. Their Kelly Street house was filled with joy. However, his mother repeated again and again wiping her tears that she would never forgive them for hurting her Benny.

❑

College Student

Benjamin started his college in September 1911 in Columbia College as a former scholar. Because he had studied so much in his two high schools and because the additional study enabled him to pass the placement exam, he started in the most advanced position possible. The best part was in all he only needed 120 marks to graduate. Benjamin set his goal for completing graduation in three years. In fact, he was about to get his diploma in only two-and-a-half years.

Speaking about his college life, Benjamin said his thoughts about college life were formed several years ago in the keen observation of the books of Frank Merriwell. Benjamin said though he had realised that Meriwell had been at Yale for a very long time, and wondered whether anyone had ever counted his semesters. Merriwell had engaged himself in every possible graduate activity except study. Yet, he added, he had always envisioned college life as the brightest period of puberty—a wonderful combination of education, friendship, romance, athletics and all kinds of enjoyable activities. However, looking back on his college career, he doesn't remember any such happy intervals, observes Benjamin. He further adds that in fact he had very few memories of his college days.

Benjamin says the most definite impression of his college days is subliminal.

Benjamin observes, "I repeatedly dream about it. Usually only a few dreams are so clear that they remain in my mind after I wake up. However a dream recurred with significant frequency during the 53 years of my life since I left Columbia College. I am a college student. I am going for a class or 'lesson', but I have written my course's schedule wrong and now I don't know where to go. I am moving from one floor to another, from one class to another, trying to figure out my place".

Benjamin further adds that in another dream he is actually in a class but hasn't prepared his work. In his dream he worries that if he is asked to read out loud then how will he manage to get out of the situation? He said that he could not sort out either of the confusions in his dream because he would inevitably wake up at some particularly difficult time. He wonders if a psychoanalyst could have deciphered these messages from his unconscious mind. However, they had little to do with the actual events of Benjamin's college career.

He recalls that his beginning at the college was not very impressive. One of his new necessary curriculum included History 'A', which was about Western Europe. Unlike most of the other students, Benjamin had already studied this while in High School and did not intend to waste any more time on it. However, it was a waking call for him when he scored 'C' in his mid-term. He, however, improved upon his performance in the next term scoring a 'B'. Comparing his time at the college, Benjamin says when he thinks about it in this perspective, his achievements seem better at present than they were at that time. Benjamin ranked second in his class and earned an honourable mention in the graduation day programme (though no awards). Benjamin wonders how he managed this successfully despite his heavy weekly syllabus and extraordinary number of jobs.

Further talking about his college days, Benjamin said he studied French from Professor Jordain, who was a Gaelic combination of boundless culture, religious scepticism and a fondness of ribald. He said it was a new phenomenon—a teacher who captivated his wit, while astonishing his Victorian scepticism. Professor Jordain was the first to be friends with Benjamin. As secretary of the *L'alliance des professeurs francaise en America*, Professor Jordain had to send programme announcements several times a year. Hence, he hired Benjamin to run addressograph, fold announcements and put them in envelopes for a decent salary of a dollar an hour. He also used to get a free ticket for the meetings. Benjamin remembers that on one such evening which was right after the war of 1914 had started, famous Yate Gilbert recited a war poem of Edmond Rostand. She was quite old at that time, however her hair was ruddy red and her voice was just as loud. Benjamin felt very impressed by her.

Benjamin recalls that one day Prof. Jordain invited him to his residence for dinner. Following the dinner he read a chapter from Gargantua by Rabelais aloud and entertained his wife and Benjamin. It was about a young mountain prince in search for the perfect toilet tissue. The professor was laughing while reading and his wife was smiling slowly in between; whereas I listened in utter embarrassment. He never understood why he could not at all be able to see the entertainment side of feces. Filth has no comic dimension to Benjamin. On the other hand, a really good porn joke has a lot to recommend. Sex is important, versatile, thrilling and therefore it perfectly embodies those incomprehensible, absurd and ridiculous provocations that make one laugh without making them feel ashamed of themselves, observes Benjamin.

Another of their French professors Camili Fonten persuaded him to participate in the annual national competition organised by a coalition of French professors. The exam for East Beach was held at Barnard College. That was the first and the only time Benjamin had entered their affiliate institution and the first and only time he found himself in a class with girls. In fact, most of the contestants on this occasion were women. The examination was divided between composition and translation or 'edition'. Benjamin says he can't remember the topic assigned to him for essay in French. However, he could never forget the translation text, which was Renan's famous 'Prayer of the Acropolis', because he made mistake in translating the first few words. He however wonders that to his surprise he won third prize in translation and honourable mention in composition.

Benjamin said he studied German literature to a great extent in college and became an expert of sorts to some extent. He did a course with Prof. Williams Edison Harvey on Goethe, Schiller and Lessing and ended it with a remarkable A+. However, in the end Benjamin lost his interest in German literature. He says that he was an admirer of German sentiments. Its combination of scientific proficiency with poetic sentimentality impressed his immature judgment and prompted him to ignore, rather forgive its sarcasm, its flattery of superiors and intimidation of subordinates. However, the period from 1914 to 1918 he developed a violent dislike for German 'Volkspsychology' and almost completely turned away from a language and literature in which he once had deep interest. He observes that perhaps in some unexplained manner he sensed the shadow of Hitler and his concentration camps behind the fiery irrationality of Fichte and the sweet 'Old Heidelberg' sentimentality of *The Student Prince*.

But, what about Latin? Benjamin says because it was one of his best subjects, he decided not to pursue it at Columbia College. He adds that if he could study it at home then what was the need to have *Horesh*, *Catullus*, *Lucretius*, and *Testis* in curriculum? He however recalls that his not studying Latin in the college created an absurd situation. He couldn't get a Bachelor of Arts degree, which required Latin in College in those days, so he became a Bachelor of Science, that too with the odd modality that he had not taken even a single science course. He recalls that when he met Dean Keppel, he was chastised for breaking a well-established college tradition.

Dean commented, “Till this date there was a saying in our college that there was only one thing certain about the Columbian Bachelor of Science degree that the graduate did not know Latin. It’s not like that anymore because of you”.

Since mathematics was his main subject, Benjamin took several courses in it. He best remembers Professor Herbert E. Hawkes, who became the Dean of the College after Keppel was made assistant secretary of war. He presented two papers in the Mathematics Colloquium. Neither of them was a great contribution and the first one cost him some money as well. It was related to Geometric Axiom. They were taught that Axioms were axioms (self-proven), but unproven. Benjamin said, considering himself a diminutive Descartes, he came up with a solution, which he believed to be a rigorous proof of the principle that a straight line is the shortest distance between two points. Professor Hawkes was very impressed and asked him to present his evidence before the Colloquium. Benjamin said, he later thought of looking at what Euclid himself had said about that Axiom. In the large commentary edition of Euclid, reserved in the University library, Benjamin found four different proofs drawn up by later mathematicians to Axiom that a straight line is the shortest distance between two points. He again felt the pain of another of his youthful dreams of greatness merge into a regrettable haze. However, there was a consolation for him that his proof was different from the four proofs given in the book. Hawkes too felt that it would still be worthwhile to present it to their group.

Benjamin also had quite an interest in philosophy. He took a first year course in formal logic, a requirement for all freshmen. Later he took Professor Fredrick A. Woodbridge’s History of Philosophy course. For an hour a week Woodbridge lectured to a sizeable number of spectators and in the second hour they would split into small quiz sections, handled by young assistants. Talking about the professor, Benjamin said Woodbridge was a remarkable lecturer listened to by the audience almost breathlessly. Remembering one of his discourses on *Kant*, he said he started his discourse with the following words :

Immanuel Kant was one of the greatest philosophers who had a wider influence on his successors than almost any other. But sometimes I wish he had never been born!

Further talking about Professor Woodbridge, Benjamin said once he began a lecture with a reference that was personally thrilling to him. The subject was Descartes and especially his famous dualism dividing the human mind and body into different universes. At this point the professor quoted Benjamin in the lecture, "In preparation to talk to you about Descartes", to which he said, "I find it difficult to get out of my mind a phrase that one of you students included in your paper on dualism. It was—'Don't let a person bind together what Descartes says below'."

Talking about his English subject and an important contribution he made to one of the classics, Benjamin said he took a famous course on the novel by Brander Mathews in English who was almost at the end of his illustrious teaching career. He said he also read John Erskine, the highly popular teacher, author (personal life of Helen of Troy) and composer. It was Erskine who once congratulated Benjamin on an observation he made in a paper on 'Wuthering Heights'. Benjamin had suggested in this paper that one reason for the alarming effect generated by that violent novel is the strange, non-British fact that no constable or any other representative of the law ever came to the scene of incidence. Erskine told him that it was a new and important contribution to the study of a masterpiece.

Further talking about his professors from Columbia College, Benjamin said another of his closest and most valuable friends at the Columbia Faculty was professor of English, Algernon Duvivier Tesin. A graduate from Harvard, he became interested in acting and toured with the well-known Julia Marlowe for several years. He wrote many plays, which unfortunately were never produced commercially. Benjamin says he learned spoken

English from Tesin. In this, the students had to read a passage and explain it clearly and conduct an intelligent debate about it. The following year Benjamin took his second course, 'Daily Theme'. Every school day, irrespective of the weather, they were required to write a one-page essay on a topic announced the day before. It was tough, however, Benjamin says, it definitely taught them how to write English.

Tesin generally liked the subjects that Benjamin chose for his topics. Near the middle of the term, he asked Benjamin to write a series of one-page character studies. He wrote about the people he knew well—his mother, his brothers, his cousin Lou and his then-girlfriend Elda.

Recalling the interaction with Tesin post character studies assignment, Benjamin said one day he called him into his office and asked, "Were all these character sketches your own work?" Amazed with the question, Benjamin replied in the affirmative. To this Tesin said, "Then I must say that you have a great gift. I have never seen such insight and such power of precision and concise expression in a man of your age". Benjamin further adds that after this Tesin remained a close personal friend to him in the ensuing years and later a financial ally during his good and bad years.

Talking about his academic career, Benjamin said the high point of his academic career was the English—History—Philosophy seminar. A small group of Honour students met once every two weeks to discuss a topic under the guidance of Erskine, Woodbridge and renowned historian James Harvey Robinson. He recalls that those were very inspiring sessions for him.

Further talking about financial assistance during his college years from September 1911 to June 1914, Benjamin says that he did a variety of jobs to take care of his college finances. He added that since his brothers contributed to the family budget, he thought he could at least earn enough for his personal and college expenses.

Speaking about those days, Benjamin adds because he tried to recount the incidents to the best of his knowledge, therefore he should mention even those incidents that caused pain to his ego. He continued that in his long professional career he had earned a reputation for conscientious integrity and that he was satisfied that the reputation has been duly earned. He says that he had deviated from the path of strict chastity only on three occasions. Recalling an incident from his childhood, Benjamin says when he was very young, he used to crave more for the sweets than what was offered to him by their strict *Mademoiselle*. He would sometimes take a coin from his mother's purse without her knowledge and exchange it with candy from the stall machine. Once the shiny coin did not fit in the stall and confused with what had happened, he brought the coin back home. It was then he found out that it was a dollar 5 piece of gold and that his mother was very upset about not finding it and was equally surprised to find it back in her purse. Benjamin said he was so rattled by the idea that he had stolen 5 dollars in place of a penny that he never did it again.

The second incident was that of the Prospect Theatre, where he worked for a short period. Recalling the incident, Benjamin said he accepted small bribes to give people better seats. Though it was a small thing, it still always bothered him, added Benjamin. He further narrates that in another attempt to earn quick money, he found a way to allow entry to eleven people with ten tickets. During a few weeks of financial crunch he used this method to earn a few dollars. However, he felt so uneasy about it that he soon stopped the practice.

Further talking about the third incident, Benjamin said his last attempt to make money by deceit was his only action in his professional career that he deeply regrets. Some land of a company in which his investment firm was interested was being acquired by the State for the purpose of road construction and they were entitled to fair compensation for the same. The State under consideration was run by the one party machine and they were told that it was necessary to hire the right firm of lawyers at a reasonable fee to get quick and satisfactory results. In such a situation, they followed the practical advice while acting like most commercial firms. Benjamin says his partner was a member of the bar, who would later get his share of the fee as a 'forwarder'. Since there was a general agreement between them to share the earning, he offered to give Benjamin half his share. Benjamin confesses he should not have accepted that money, but he did and has regretted it ever since.

Learning from his experiences, Benjamin says his weaknesses led him to be somewhat tolerant of embezzlement by relatives, friends, fellow employees, or even his own employees. He adds wherever their theft was driven by enormous financial pressure, he felt pity rather than reproach. However, he adds, he feels only contempt for the rich who are dishonest out of habit, greed or outright perversion; as well as for those who abuse a position of trust and respect.

Further talking about the jobs he had undertaken during his college years, Benjamin said at the end of his first year of college a friend stopped by the theatre to talk to him. He had just started a wonderful job where he was paid 40 dollars a month for regular daytime hours and 50 dollars a month for night shifts. They needed more college students and his friend thought this job would be good for Benjamin. The amount of money was enough to raise his interest. After a brief interview he got an appointment for the night shift which ran from 4 pm in the evening till midnight, six days a week. The company was US Express Company and his boss, M.A. Fischer was the competency specialist.

Speaking about his new job, Benjamin said this work was supposed to mark an important stage in his development. The Interstate Commerce Commission had set a completely new basis for express rates across the country by a block method to replace the complex station-to-station rates. The companies protested, saying the new system would ruin them. They were preparing an elaborate demonstration to support their protest.

Discussing the happenings, Benjamin said four other big express companies—Adams, American, Southern and Well Fargo—were hand-crafting their displays in the traditional way. However, Mr. Fischer had sold the US Express on the new punch card or Hollerith method for rapidly sorting and tabulating complex data. The Hollerith machines were leased by the Computing-Tabulating-Recording Corporation, a poorly-funded and poorly-regarded company. Its stocks were said to represent nothing but water and could be worth 3 million dollars in the market. Benjamin had never thought that he would see the stocks of that company, which was to be renamed 'International Business Machines' one day selling for billions of dollars on the New York Stock Exchange.

Speaking about his job and Mr. Fischer, Benjamin said the US Express project was established at a rental location at 76, Washington Street. He found the broader aspects of his work very interesting, although the actual physical labour was essentially monotonous. One of his colleagues and Colombian classmate, Lou Bernstein was equally interested in the project. Bernstein along with Benjamin used to discuss work with Mr. Fischer, who was so pleased with their interest in his ideas that on one Sunday afternoon he invited them to his house for a long discussion. Benjamin said their discussions were to have quite unexpected consequences for Mr. Fischer and for them.

Benjamin continues that it was September 1912 and with that began his second year at Colombia. He continued his job attending classes for about twenty-one hours per week and also doing homework. Bernstein also began working in the night shift and hence they both worked together at the company. One evening a surprising rumour reached them that Fischer had resigned after a squabble with the chief auditor over some violation of company rules by his assistant. Both Benjamin and Bernstein wondered about this very special project. However, they didn't have to wait long. Mr. Tait, the general auditor of the company came to their room and expressed his desire to meet Bernstein and

Grossbaum. He was told that they both had a good sense of the job and asked if that was true. They answered in affirmation without any hesitation. Then he asked them to meet him in his office after the midnight shift.

Benjamin said they had a short and exciting conversation in Mr. Tait's office. He asked them what they thought about taking Fischer's place and taking over the project? And whether they could start the preparations immediately and complete every step of the process by the next evening? The two of them replied in affirmation. The next question, however, was not that simple. Mr. Tait asked if Benny Grossbaum could arrange to apply for leave at the college, take day shifts, and assume primary responsibility for the job? To this Benjamin replied that he would have to consult Dean Keppel on the matter and also asked that the compensation for the job should be adequate. Both Bernstein and Benjamin agreed to return to Mr. Tait's office the next night at 10 o'clock after completing the necessary work.

Recalling the thrill of the offer, Benjamin said the next day passed like a brilliant dream. When he told his story to Dean Keppel, he became equally excited and told Benjamin, "Sure, Ben, take this leave. If you can prepare well enough to pass the semester exam, I'll see you get marks for your current courses".

After the discussion with the Dean, both of them then started working on the outline of the project. They were at Mr. Tait's office exactly at 10 o'clock with their charts. He looked at it without much consideration as he had never mastered the intricacies of the project. However, their logical arrangement of different stages impressed him and he was clearly relieved with the current situation. Mr. Tait then repeated his questions from the previous night and both Bernstein and Benjamin replied in affirmation. He then asked Benjamin, "How much salary do you want to take charge of the job?" He looked straight into Mr. Tait's eyes and said, "You have to double my current salary, sir". He immediately agreed to the condition.

Soon after the demand Benjamin realised that his request for 100 dollars a month was too modest; however, it was too late to change anything now. Bernstein agreed on a 50 per cent increase in his current salary, or 75 dollars a month. Also, he was not required to take a break from college.

Benjamin held his high position for four-and-a-half months. Though he thought that he did not work very efficiently, yet Bernstein and he understood the technical problems quite well. Soon after they took office, two new faces—Greiner and Ryan—showed up with them. They were brought in by Mr. Tait to be taught in depth about the project and the responsibilities therein. Both Benjamin and Bernstein were not happy with the newcomers and considered it a shrewd move on the part of Mr. Tait.

A little later in response to Vice President Platt's dissatisfaction with their rate of progress, Tait decided that they would run three shifts. Two of which would be run by Benjamin—from 8 am to 4 pm and then midnight to 8 am. It was considered that after all he was young and could bear the strain of these shifts.

As work progressed, Greiner and Ryan's team began to assert more and more authority over Benjamin and Bernstein. Towards the end of the project, they had actually taken over the actual direction of the work and Bernstein and Benjamin were limited to overseeing some of the work and offering advice on some technical questions. By the end of January their work was finished and Benjamin received his last salary together with a cold goodbye.

Disappointed with his last days in the job he rushed for, Benjamin said that he had plenty of time to prepare to return to college in the last month on his job. In keeping with Dean Keppel's suggestions he decided to take several exams for the current semester in English, French, German and Maths. Just before he left the college, he had started economics; nevertheless weeks of exposure to 'dismal science', it had failed to pique his interest. Little did he know that later on he was going to make his lifelong career in the branch of economics called 'Finance' and become a professor of this subject in two of his big universities.

Coming back to his family's financial situation, Benjamin said suddenly another financial disaster hit their family. His eldest brother Leon had long been eager to rise above his position as the chinaware salesman at Wanamaker and was attracted by the possibilities of the burgeoning film industry. He wanted to purchase a small theatre in Jamaica, Long Island for 1500 dollars. Their mother borrowed 1000 dollars from her rich sister and Benjamin paid the remaining amount from his savings. Leon's venture proved to be a complete failure and in a few months all the money was lost. Benjamin was left neither with money nor any job. Remembering an open promise made by Mr. Tait at the time of his being relieved from the job to seek him if Benjamin ever needed a job in future, Benjamin immediately wrote to him explaining his plight and requested him for a part-time job. His secretary replied that Mr. Tait was sorry because hiring part-timers was against the company policies which is why they could not do anything for him. It was a bitter lesson for Benjamin. He said he would never trust anyone in future for their open promises to help. Benjamin looked everywhere for work but failed. Finally out of desperation he accepted the task of selling coupons for cut-rate photos from door-to-door. Benjamin said no work could have been more humiliating than what he was doing.

Benjamin remembers the day when he returned home and fell on the bed and burst into tears inconsolably. His mother quietly came inside the room and took him in her arms and said, "I am sure things will be fine soon". Her support gave courage to Benjamin and thinking about Tait's refusal to fulfil his promise, he wrote directly to Mr. Platt, the acting president of the US Express Company. He told him about his story in as dignified and touching language as he could. Benjamin received his reply saying that in view of the special circumstances he would relax the company rules for him. He was offered the job for half day as a waybills checker for 25 dollars a month and to continue the same full-time during the summer holidays. With this reply from Mr. Platt, Benjamin felt as if his life had been saved.

While speaking about his new job at the old place, Benjamin said one day he was busy with his work when he felt some movement in the room. He saw a group of corporate executives entering the room along with a short but stern-looking man that they didn't recognise. The man was Mr. Roberts who was recently elected as the president of the company. He was brought in because the directors of the company had decided to liquidate the business.

Three years after Roberts took over as the President, the company went into liquidation. By then Benjamin had completed his college and started working as an employee of a New York Stock Exchange firm. One day his boss told him, "Ben, to my knowledge, US Express still owns 1,00,000 dollars of the Lehigh Valley Railroad Perpetual 6s". He asked Benjamin to go and meet president Roberts and find out what he was going to do with them. This new relationship with Roberts attracted Benjamin's ego and he hurriedly put on his hat and reached Roberts' office.

This hurried action cost some embarrassment to Benjamin when he asked Roberts about the Lehigh Valley. He told Benjamin that he considered selling them and asked him for a quotation. Benjamin had neglected the elementary precaution of checking the market for bond price before meeting Roberts and hence was embarrassed with the question. He somehow managed to get out of the situation by giving some nonsensical excuse. Learning his lesson, Benjamin never attended any business interview without proper preparations.

Further talking about the jobs he undertook, Benjamin recalled that he had also tutored the children of army officers including the son of famous General Leonard Wood who lived with his family on Governor's Island.

Flushed talking about the subject, Benjamin said there was also the small issue of sex. He said although he was mature in intellect at that time, yet was considered to be an imbecile when it came to girls and love. Nonetheless, he had the same curiosity as other children and since he read more than other children, comparatively he had enough book knowledge about the subject. However it was also true that he was way behind other boys when it came down to actual experience.

Further talking on the subject, Benjamin said he met a girl named Rose through his cousin Helen. However he could still never gather the courage to put his hand around her waist while dancing to the tunes of '*Yee Old Mill* in Coney Island'. Benjamin said Rose married someone else and he wrote a poem in her memory that can be found in his collection of 'Versions and Verse'.

Benjamin said his eldest brother developed an interest in Sylvia Mazur who lived in Bath Beach, Brooklyn. However, when Sylvia got engaged to a certain Armand, Leon started dating her younger sister Hazel. Hazel was beautiful and intelligent and had remarkable poise and practical knowledge of all kinds, added Benjamin. He added that Hazel was full of life and ambitious and earned quite a substantial amount of money by teaching dance and elocution to neighbouring children as well as some adults. She was benevolent, helpful and a decent person in every sense.

Benjamin said soon Leon felt the need of introducing his famous younger brother to Hazel. One Sunday he went with Leon to Hazel's house. She came to greet them and Benjamin and Hazel got interested in each other. This, he said was a moment of the shortest experience of romance he ever felt. Hence he became a regular visitor to her house.

Speaking about his first focused romance, Benjamin said he was 19 when his friend and co-worker Lou Bernstein introduced him to Elda. He said though she was not as beautiful as Hazel, yet she had a very lively and interesting face. A romance soon blossomed between the two. Benjamin said he started meeting her every day at L Station on his way back from work. Remembering his time with Elda, he said there was a courtyard behind her house where a swing hung from a tree. Further remembering a fragrant evening in that courtyard, Benjamin said he was sitting on that swing next to Elda talking some nonsense when he felt her hand on his neck. Recalling the incident, he felt his face moving towards hers. However it took him too long to realise that she wanted him to kiss her.

Benjamin confessed that following this day they were definitely in love. He further added that every time they met after that nature urged their bodies to become one. But it never happened because it would not be respectable added Benjamin. He said one Sunday afternoon Elda sat on his lap among the crowd of young people at her house—an act he would have loved to do alone. However at that time she looked ridiculous to him doing such a thing in front of all his friends. On top of it she asked in a loud voice, "Ben don't you love me?" To which Benjamin replied in a whisper, "Of course I do, dear". However she kept insisting, "But tell me that you love me more than anything in the world. Tell everyone". In the spur of that moment Benjamin said yes he loved her the most.

However, thinking about what had happened, Benjamin sent a long, prudent letter to Elda the next evening. He reasoned that he was still in college and would probably spend three years in law school after graduation. He said how could they seriously think about love if marriage had to be postponed till he was capable enough to take proper care of her. After many arguments and excuses, Benjamin announced his sad decision—they should end their romance immediately and it would be wise if they did not meet again.

Confessing about his romantic life, Benjamin said his relationship with Elda and later with a less interesting girl paved the way for the main romantic chapter of his youth in which he married Hazel. They had five children together. Benjamin said they shared successes and sorrows, nonetheless in the end they were also divorced.

He said he and Hazel had almost everything to offer to each other, yet they lacked the necessary knowledge about themselves and that proved fatal to their marriage.

❑

The Beginning of His Career

The final month of Benjamin's college was full of career opportunities for him. First and foremost was the invitation from Professor Woodbridge, head of the Department of Philosophy, who called Benjamin to have lunch with him at the Faculty Club. Woodbridge offered him to stay in the Columbia College as a member of the Department of Philosophy. This invitation was followed by another proposal similar to this one from Professor Hawkes from the Department of Mathematics. Benjamin recalls that following these two invitations the third one was a total surprise for him as it came from the great Professor Erskine who invited him to his office for a chat. He told Benjamin that he would be a valuable addition to the English Department and that the career at the University would be the most favourable for him.

Benjamin says it was natural for him to be happy to get so many offers and be surprised at the same time. However, when he spoke to Dean Keppel about these opportunities, he advised Benjamin not to be hasty in taking any decisions and that to take his own time. Benjamin said Dean Keppel had a strong tendency to advise college students to venture into business rather than locking them into the ivory tower of academic life. He said he thought that may be the Dean might find some interesting work for him too.

However, when Benjamin met the Dean on the campus a few days later, he told Benjamin that he tried to contact him yesterday over the phone, but was unable to get in touch. Dean added that he had a very interesting opportunity for him. Benjamin asked, "What was the opportunity". Dean Keppel replied, "Sir Norman Angel - you know him, author of *The Great Illusion* - was in my office. He was leaving this morning on a new peacekeeping mission that would be carried out across Europe. He asked me for a young assistant and I recommended your name. However, he had to leave without you".

Perturbed over the missed opportunity to be on an extraordinary tour in the company of such a distinguished author and person, Benjamin felt really disappointed. He decided he would contemplate the strangeness of fate over the missed telephone call later. However, about two months later the First World War broke out. Benjamin thought that if he had not missed the opportunity of going on the tour he would have been in England with Angel at that time and as a British subject he would have been under military call and would probably have been fighting in the Flanders regions. He thought that it would have been an iconic conclusion to his peace mission.

Talking about his venture with advertising, Benjamin said one of his friends Freddie Swed ran a small advertising agency and thought writing advertising copies could be challenging career for him. He suggested that Benjamin should join his office for a modest salary on a trial basis. Benjamin thought of trying this since he still had some time. The advertising agency's main account was with Carbona. It was the famous non-flammable cleaning fluid. Benjamin was ready to come up with the slogan and other advertising ideas and his first attempt was—"Carbona removes stains from everything". Benjamin said after a few other similar attempts, he produced a masterpiece—a limerick, which he still remembers very well:

There was a young girl in Winona
Who had never heard of Carbona,
She started cleaning
With a can of Benzene,
And now her poor parents mourn over her.

Thrilled over his limerick, when Benjamin showed it to Swed, he was as excited as only an advertising person could be. He immediately put on his hat and went to Carbona's office to show Benjamin's gem to President Weinstein. Benjamin, holding his breath, nervously waited for his friend's return. He returned in half an hour with a sad face. Benjamin asked what he was sad about, "Did Weinstein not like his limerick?" Freddie replied that he did like it very much and went crazy laughing. However, he told me it wouldn't do, added Freddie. Surprised by the reply, Benjamin asked the reason for the refusal. Freddie replied that Weinstein felt that his entire campaign was directed towards intimidating people to buy Carbona and this would make them laugh and cancel the rest of their copy. Sympathising with Benjamin, Freddie said it was too bad because he liked it.

Benjamin thought he did not know whether Weinstein's decision about his limerick was better than Swed's. However he did know that he felt very disappointed with his advertising copy writing career and was prepared to consider more trustworthy business ideas than this.

Further speaking about his final days at the college, Benjamin said he had competed in Columbia College for a mathematical award. The prize money for the award was 150 dollars a year, which was no small amount those days. He remembers that probably there were five contestants for the competition. His cousin Lou had also won that during his graduation year and hence his family assumed that he too would win the award too. However, it so happened that his friend J.J. Tanjola won the award who used to eat and sleep maths and who went on to become mathematics professor later in his life. Benjamin was the runner-up.

Benjamin further said that he found on his commencement day event that he was also the runner-up for the award given to the graduate with the best Grade Point Average in his entire college career. Benjamin recalls that his only consolation was the honourable mention under the name of the winner.

He said despite all these setbacks he had the privilege of being elected to '*Phi Beta Kappa*' that was a very prestigious honour. He added that it was going to benefit him in his later life in one way or the other.

Speaking about the commencement day, Benjamin said on the opening day just before the event, he was called again to Dean Keppel's office. A member of the New York Stock Exchange had come to visit the Dean about his son's very poor grade and while having the conversation he asked the Dean to recommend one of his best students for appointment as a bond seller. Dean gave his name to Mr. Neuberger with an encouraging recommendation. Dean believed that the Wall Street College presented great opportunities for the students and that Benjamin should seriously consider this career rather than college teaching.

Recalling the meeting, Benjamin said he agreed to meet Mr. Neuberger and an appointment was made for the following day for 3:15 pm after he returned from the exchange. The name of his firm was Neuberger, Henderson and Loeb and the office address was—100 Broadway.

Benjamin said he clearly remembers that he arrived early and was waiting in front of the clock of Trinity Church. He then crossed the street and entered a tight space on the ground floor of the American Surety building. He was then taken to Mr. Samuel Neuberger's (Mr. SN) office. He was an attractive stout man with white hair who seemed very old to Benjamin, though he was not actually more than 50 years old. After some general remarks he referred him to his younger brother Mr. Alfred H. Neuberger (Mr. AN) for his actual interview, added Benjamin.

Speaking about the younger Neuberger, Benjamin said Mr. AN, whom he soon learned was the *de facto* senior member and guide of the firm, was tall and handsome like his older brother with an exception that he had brown hair. He spoke with great seriousness and authority. Benjamin said he asked him about his studies in economics and that he had to admit that he had completely dropped the subject mainly because of his job with the US Express Company. However, Benjamin satisfied Mr. AN when he said that he knew the difference between stocks and bonds. Mr. AN told him that despite his lack of specific training, they would take him because of the recommendation of Dean Keppel. He asked Benjamin about his general financial position to which he replied that it was weak and that he had to depend on his salary for a livelihood.

To this Mr. AN said that they always gave 10 dollars a week in the beginning to young people joining them. However considering his needs he would increase this amount to 12 dollars. He said that it would take some time for Benjamin to make money selling bonds with them.

Benjamin remembers that Mr. AN talked about how there were great opportunities in Wall Street for the right person. Benjamin only knew about this in rumours and novels as a place of drama and excitement and felt inspired to participate in its mystical rituals and important events. He accepted all the terms and agreed to start from next week. As Benjamin was getting up to leave, Mr. AN raised a long finger in the air and said with authoritative seriousness, "One final warning young man! If you guess you will lose your money. Always remember that". The interview ended with these somewhat scary words, hence deciding Benjamin's lifelong career.

Benjamin said his arrangement with the firm was that he would spend a few weeks in the back office as a runner and general helper to learn the business from scratch. After that he would go to the bond department and learn how to sell bonds. Benjamin said during those days Wall Street was not as organised as it is today and there was more exchange of buy-sell slips, delivery of securities, cheques, certification and similar messenger works. He learned a lot there—first in the delivery department, then in the order room and later in the bookkeeping department.

Amazed with the workings of the Wall Street, Benjamin said the financial industry's unusual way of handling large sums of money surprised him. Explaining the working, Benjamin said when a cheque was certified and ready to be returned, the clerk would call 'Neuberger' or 'Content' or whatever other name it was. A runner would go to the window and say 'cheque for Neuberger' and a piece of paper, probably for 5 million dollars, was handed over to him – without anyone asking for identification. Even more shocking was the careless disposal of Stock Certificates, he added. He continued that he would be getting out of the lift to deliver when another runner would come to him and ask, "Are you going to Sartorius?" When he replied yes, the runner would hand him a parcel of certificates and ask him to deliver them too for him at the Sartorius.

Benjamin said he was surprised to see how cost-effective the rich can be despite the large casual dealings in the brokerage business. He said sometimes when he was in Mr. KN's office for some work he would see him sending cheques to pay personal bills. For this purpose he used self-addressed stamped envelopes obtained from corporations for the proxy of his annual meeting. Mr. AN would write a new address by striking off the address of the corporation and thus would save a ticket of 2 cents. According to him, continued Benjamin, there was no point in letting the envelopes and tickets go waste. This display of frugality by such a wealthy man not only shocked him but also hurt him as he had great respect for AN's intelligence and acumen, he added.

Almost half-a-century had elapsed since those experiences. Benjamin recalls that after some serious financial woes in the middle, he had amassed a considerable amount of money—far more than his Wall Street employers. He said over time he gained a better understanding of the monetary psychology of rich people.

The basic fact is that our attitude towards wealth is determined in early life by innate disposition, conditions of existence and certain key experiences. A person who is extravagant initially is likely to remain as it is—only in different types subject to unforeseen events, which constrain his expenditure, he added. Benjamin continued that if anyone goes from poverty to wealth, he easily casts off the shackles of the initial compulsions and becomes a free spender.

Speaking about the teachings on handling finances Benjamin said most of the children come into the world without strong instincts in matters of finance. Their attitude and their future behaviour is largely determined by the initial environment in their homes. Even if their family is affluent, they can be trained in the habits of careful and economical spending by example, teaching and discipline. They can learn these habits at a young age while handling small amounts—usually their weekly allowance. He continues that later inheriting the huge wealth unbalances their attitude. They show extreme care and frivolity in small matters, while in big matters they tend to be careless, generous and personally extravagant. Of course, people who are born wealthy and raised in an environment of generosity tend to adapt to their circumstances without much difficulty.

Quoting his own example, Benjamin said a typical poor boy-rich man like himself used to be ridiculously inconsistent in spending. He can be easy even extravagant, of all large outlays, whereas in small expenses he can fight a constant war against the inherent insignificance. Benjamin continues that in his own case the motivation for such skimping is governed by two counter-intuitive factors. He said firstly he became aware of the problem and was determined to use his intelligence and will power to solve it as far as possible. Secondly, he continued, he is extremely sensitive to how others react to his conduct. He said he is ashamed to succumb to his economical instincts in front of his neighbours if he senses someone is watching him.

Citing his own example, Benjamin says, however, when he is alone sometimes he just relaxes and does silly and cheap things inspired from his childhood adaptations. For example, he always uses taxis when he is with someone in New York. However, when he is alone, he often takes the metro and gives two excuses to himself for doing so. First, the roads are so crowded that the metro would move faster than the cabs. Second, he can read in the metro whereas he cannot do that in a taxi. Even so, believe it or not, he can avoid buying a newspaper saying that carrying it would be a hassle. Perhaps this reluctance to spend small sums is attributable to the fact that he had never smoked or indulged in alcohol.

Explaining an important aspect of the Stock Exchange-Curb Market, Benjamin observed like all newcomers to the Wall Street, he was also deeply influenced by the Curb Market. At that time it was located on Brand Street and occupied a roped-off area of about 20 square yards. The Curb brokers used to congregate there in all weather conditions to conduct their business in the open air. Although the Curb Market was less important than the New York Stock Exchange, yet several important corporations were listed in it. Benjamin continued that often the business used to go very high involving several million dollars in a single day. In spite of strange physical arrangements, the Market was handled with reasonable efficiency, he added.

Speaking about his days at the firm, Benjamin said after working for about four weeks as a runner, he was moved to the Bond department. Before he moved there, the people working in the Bond department included two young but relatively experienced Bond salesmen. One was Daniel Loeb, nephew of the firm partner Jack Loeb, who was hard-working and a very serious person, and the other was Harold Rouse. Harold's motto was, "Never do for yourself what you can get someone else to do for you".

Talking about his work in the new department Benjamin said he had a two-fold task there—to learn everything he could about the Bond and to make himself as useful as possible to the department. He said even in his spare time he took his task of self-education very seriously. He bought a notebook and on each page of the notebook he wrote key statistics about every Bond issue that was given in a way that it was convenient for him to remember it. Benjamin said even after all these years he still remembers that black notebook and some of the entries written in it.

Talking about a small unrest in Europe in July 1914 Benjamin said that month the prince of Austria was murdered in Sarajevo, Bosnia leading to serious skirmishes between Vienna and Little Serbia. However, the New York Stock Market paid no attention to this European tension and continued with its business. It was at this time that Benjamin's '*Phi Beta Kappa*' key arrived. Very proud of it, he hung it on the chain of the watch he wore on his neck. Lester Neuberger, the youngest member of the firm was impressed by the honour bestowed upon an employee of his firm. An hour later he said to Benjamin that, "Ben, can I ask a *Phi Beta Kappa* guy to run and get me a pack of cigarettes?" Benjamin said he went out with the key swinging in the chain around his neck.

Speaking about an indestructible memory of calm period before the Victorian world going up in flames and the belated end of the nineteenth century, Benjamin said the Australian Tennis team had challenged the Americans for the Davis Cup. One of the Neuberger partners had two tickets for the third day's match; however he wouldn't be able to make it to the match. Therefore, he gifted those tickets to Benjamin who invited sedentary tennis enthusiast Fred Greenman to join him for the match. They then left for Forest Hills Stadium to watch the match. Australia was leading by splitting the singles and winning the doubles on the first day. Now, Norman Brooks, veteran of the Australian team, was to face young Norris Williams who had recently graduated from Harvard. Norris was Greenman's classmate at Harvard. Benjamin said it was this match that brought tennis out of its past of tea party, tenderness, polite applause into a new era of excitement, incitement and uncontrollable spirit with its tremendous theatrics.

Then came the time of torment when the deadly fire broke out in early August 1914, said Benjamin. This raised some questions for Benjamin like—Will it lead to the extinction of Western Civilisation? Was it the result of a lack of competent leadership or diplomatic skills among the patriarchs of Europe? Or was it just another war in the endless series between nations, which ultimately leaves no major historical mark but are disastrous for those who fight them and unfortunate for those who survive it? Benjamin said it would be hardly appropriate to mention his reflection on these questions here; while others have thought more deeply and thoroughly about these problems than him. Therefore he would only state this from a narrow point of view of a young New Yorker who had experienced the same nervousness and excitement as his neighbours in the early stages of the play.

Speaking about the impact of the war on the Stock Market, Benjamin said a few days before August 3, there was great panic in the Stock Market but not the state of dread. However, the actual break of hostilities shocked the financial community both here and in Europe. The New York Stock Market was overwhelmed by the terrible wave of billing which was soon followed by the Governors' decision to close the New York Stock Exchange. All other Stock Exchanges immediately followed suit. The flood of sales may seem strange and illogical to those who were only familiar with the boom of war that was soon to come. The explanation, though, was both technical and simple. He explained, European investors were in possession of sizeable amounts of American securities. When the war broke out, their first concern was to bring his money home. They instinctively, though wrongly, as they later realised, felt that their wealth would be safe with them rather than in a distant land during the time of conflict. This sudden and overwhelming response from foreign holders put an intolerable strain on the local market, which during those days took their psychological cues from the daily dealings of the London Exchange.

Recalling those times, Benjamin said he still sees those headlines clearly in his mind—Austria declared war on Serbia; Russia declared war on Austria; Germany declared war on Russia; France declared war on Germany; Britain declared war on Germany. It was all so hard to believe and yet so horrifyingly true. Uncertain about his future financial situation, he said when the exchanges closed, he was wondering what would happen to their business and his job as nothing was really going on at Wall Street. However, all the firms retained their employees on lower wages. Benjamin was glad that he still had his job even if for 10 dollars a week.

Benjamin continued that a few months later the markets reopened on a trading committee basis allowing transactions at a low price than what it was earlier. War orders soon began pouring in from the French and British and the economic picture soon turned from gloom to boom. Trading restrictions were lifted and the great wartime boom began in the Stock Market. In this sudden upheaval, their firm struggled with lack of helpers as their workers had left during the closure of the market. As a result of this he was called to serve on various fronts. Benjamin adds that on some active days he helped his boardboys to put up Stock Quotations, while on other days he used to operate the telephone switch board or help various clerks in the back office. He even went out to make significant deliveries of securities from time to time and his salary came back to its previous figure of 12 dollars a week.

Speaking about his duties with the firm, Benjamin said after some time he resumed his activities in the Bond department and soon he was out and about meeting clients. It was a very pleasant business compared to his previous endeavours as a salesman for cut-rate photo coupons or shirt-board advertising. He said it seems that the visit from a Bond salesman satisfies the ego of the average businessman and that his 'no' was always polite.

Continuing about his job at the firm, Benjamin said during these early days when he started going out he met one Mr. Richard Willstatter. He was the floor member of the New York Stock Exchange who had rented a desk in their Bond department. He came every afternoon after the market closed for the day and spent some time at his table. Mr. Willstatter soon developed an interest in him. On a few occasions, Mr. Willstatter took him to Republican Club luncheons which were addressed by prominent people. On one such occasion Ambassador Von Bernstorff tried to speak in favour of Germany, but without much success. On another occasion the Japanese ambassador told them why his country had entered the war siding his allies. Benjamin said it was his pleasure to hear from the then Mayor of New York, John Mitchell about his successful fight against Tammany Hall. Tragically three years later he had to be a part of the Guard of Honour at the Mayor's funeral.

Benjamin further elaborates about his work that in connection of his Bond assignment, he began to study the Railroad Report in detail. He devoted himself wholeheartedly to reading *Principles of Bond Investing* written by Lawrence Chamberlain which was the standard textbook on the subject. Based on these studies he got an idea to write an analysis of the Missouri Pacific Railroad. A report for the year ended June 1914 convinced him that it was in a poor physical and dangerous financial condition and that investors would not hold on to their Bonds. When his report was complete on the subject, he showed it to his friend Willstatter who liked it and in turn showed it to a partner of JS Bash & Company. He said Bach's people told him that they would like to have him in their statistical department if he was interested. By that time he was convinced that he would rather be a statistician than a salesman. Therefore he went to see Mr. Morton Stern, who later went on to become an important partner in the Bach

Firm. He offered him 18 dollars a week to work for them, to prepare reports and answering inquiries provided his current firm raised no objections.

Benjamin said everything was great! He was pretty sure that NH & L would be happy to get rid of him because he was not bringing in any Bond sales commissions to earn his 12 dollars a week salary. However, when he told Mr. Samuel Neuberger about his decision to change jobs, the result was contradictory to what he had expected. How could he have been so treacherous as to even think of leaving them after all they had done for him? How could the other firm have the courage to steal one of their employees? That was against the rules of the Stock Exchange.

Hearing their response, Benjamin said, "But I felt that I am not working worth my salary". On this Mr. Samuel Neuberger said, "It's for us to decide, not for you". "But I don't want to be a Bond salesman. I am sure I can do better as a statistician", he replied. Mr. Neuberger said, "It is time now that we should have a statistics department", and asked him if he could be that while working with their firm. Benjamin replied that if they really wanted him to stay with them he would be happy to do so. Mr. Neuberger said that they would discuss his salary and would let him know about it.

Benjamin said after a firm meeting it was decided that they would pay him a weekly salary of 15 dollars. He was happy to settle on their offer and start his genuine and definitive career exclusively as a security analyst. Then, a few months later when the business was thriving, SN called him to tell that from now on he would be getting 18 dollars a week so that he would not feel like he was missing out on being with their firm. This ended the Bach incident in his career. However, a few months later when he got another increment, SN told him with trepidation that the firm had resolved that if he accepted the other offer, they would never hire a college student again.

Speaking about Mr. Willstatter, Benjamin said after some time his benefactor changed the place and their meetings became less frequent. Although he called him to meet, Benjamin said he was too busy with his new work that he could not go. However, once he saw Mr. Willstatter on the road and felt guilty for ignoring him and changed his course of path. Nevertheless, the next time they met on the way, Mr. Willstatter reprimanded him for the gross indecency of not even bowing his head in respect the last time they crossed each other. Benjamin said he felt very ashamed of himself and admitted it openly, which Mr. Willstatter took in good spirit. He said that this little incident taught him something. He realised that if one has failed in performing his duty towards someone, there is a natural tendency to isolate oneself from them, which hurts them even more. For fair and friendly behaviour one must admit and correct their mistake at the very first opportunity.

❑

Initial Years at Wall Street

Benjamin was destined to spend his entire professional life—42 years—at Wall Street, a journey that he began as a runner of a brokerage house that culminated in him becoming one of the heads of a thriving investment fund and the chairmanship of two major business ventures. Over the years at Wall Street he had learned a lot from the teaching and examples of others. However, what he learned had never stopped him from making minor mistakes of his own and neither had it contributed much to whatever success he had achieved.

Benjamin said he took a central pedagogical approach, grounded in practical considerations to Wall Street. His school training had made him investigative, reflective and critical towards things. Later, he was able to add two other qualities to the existing ones that are usually not accompanied by theoretical leanings—first, an intuition of what is important in a problem or situation, and the ability to avoid wasting time on the unnecessary; and second, an innate tendency to pragmatism, to get things done, to find solutions, and especially to develop new approaches and techniques.

Speaking about his talents and luck, Benjamin said if he was fortunate in the assortment of talents he brought to financial analysis, he was equally fortunate in the era in which he entered Wall Street. He continued that when he started at Wall Street, investing was almost entirely limited to Bonds only. Though, common stocks, with a few exceptions, were primarily viewed as vehicles of speculations. Nevertheless, a considerable amount of window dressing had started to be placed around the common stocks that were considered to be closely related to gambling casinos to give some aura of respect to them. He further added that the corporations started to provide detailed information on operations and finances either voluntarily or in line with stock exchange requirements. Financial services began to feature this material in convenient forms in their manuals and current publications. In addition, he added, regulatory bodies such as the Inter-State Commerce Commission and various State Public Utility Commissions were collecting a massive amount of data about railroads and gas and power companies. All this data was open to inspection and study.

Speaking about the impact of World War I, Benjamin said in the year 1914 this mass of financial information was largely being lost in the field of common stock analysis. The figures were not overlooked; however they were being studied superficially and with marginal interest. He said what mattered most was the variety of internal information, some of which pertained to business operations, new orders, anticipated profits, etc. Yet, more than that was the importance related to the current activities and plans of the market manipulators.

Further speaking about what positive came out of World War I, Benjamin said for a number of reasons including improvement in the financial power of large industrial companies due to World War I, after 1914 the importance of intrinsic value and investing power were bound to increase in common stock analysis. He said as a newcomer who was unfettered by the warped conventions of the old regime, he could have easily adapted to the new forces that were beginning to enter the financial landscape. Benjamin said he learned to distinguish between the important and uninteresting, the trustworthy and untrustworthy, the honest and the dishonest, with greater clarity and better judgment than many of his superiors whose intelligence was clouded by their experiences. He continued that therefore to a great extent he found Wall Street an intact area to be tested by a real, penetrating analysis of security values. He said with his good fortune of internal equipment and favourable tides he could hardly have missed being successful. Nevertheless his career had suffered more than one setback.

Remembering his time with the NH&L firm, Benjamin said he would begin with a small example—among the clients of Neuberger, Henderson and Loeb was the aged Mr. Warner who was forced to take a job with them as he had to leave his stock exchange firm due to bad business. Mr. Warner, who was never seen walking without his stick, knew the final quote on any stock and every bit of information and rumour going around in the street with absolute certainty. Mr. Warner once convinced him to walk on the street with the stick, which he did, but only for a short period of time.

Further talking about Mr. Warner, Benjamin said it was the year 1915 and he was helping in the client room as a boardboy. He used to exchange comments on topics such as financial development and corporate income with Mr. Warner there. It was the time when Missouri, Kansas and Texas railroads were showing some improvement in their profits. However, their stock (called 'kitty') was selling for a low 12 dollars a share. Benjamin said he might have helped Mr. Warner in a case some time. In return for that he suggested jointly buying 100 shares of Kitty Common Stock and that he would invest his money and take a share from Benjamin later. He readily accepted the offer. However, soon Mr. AN came to know about the matter as he knew everything about everyone in the office. He called Benjamin to his office and gave him a piece of his mind. Mr. AN reminded him of the piece of advice he had given earlier against speculation and then said in a particularly contemptuous tone, "If you were about to speculate regarding something then at least you should have been more sensible than to choose that useless laid-off rail road like MKT." Benjamin said he soon ended the feud immediately by selling his shares at a small profit. He said after this episode he could only imagine the reprimand AN would have given to the respected Mr. Warner.

Speaking about the real beginning of his career at Wall Street, Benjamin said his career as a Wall Street operator of a certain kind actually happened in the year 1915 with the liquidation plans of Guggenheim Exploration Company. The company had major interests in several important copper mines—Nevada, Chino, Ray Consolidated, and Utah—that once actively traded on the New York Stock Exchange. When Guggenheim proposed to dissolve and distribute its various holdings to its shareholders, Benjamin calculated that the aggregate current market value of its various holdings would be much greater than the price of Guggenheim shares. Hence, an arbitrage profit was practically assured in buying the Guggenheim shares as well as selling the Chino, Nevada, Ray and Utah shares. However, the potential risks, he thought, were –

1. Failure of the shareholders to approve the liquidation.
2. Long delay due to litigation or other difficulties.
3. Difficulty in maintaining short positions in shares sold till they were actually distributed to Guggenheim stockholders.

Benjamin said none of these risks seemed big enough to him. He then recommended operations from the firm, which arbitrated a fair number of shares. He also recommended it to other people in the office. He said he remembered that Harold Rouse proposed that he should take over the entire operation for him in exchange of 20 per cent share in the profit. In this way, he said, he conducted his very first arbitration—an operation which was to prove one of his special areas of research and action. The liquidation plan was completed without any hindrance and the profit was exactly as it was calculated. Everyone was happy—even Benjamin.

Speaking of his growth in the Stock Market, Benjamin said the year 1915-16 saw the Big Bull Market of the First World War. The United States of America was not yet involved as a participant; however it benefited greatly from orders for war supplies and supply orders from Britain and France. Common stock prices that had collapsed with the break out of war rose to exponential levels. The business of the firm increased. Benjamin said apart from being a statistician or security analyst and financial paper writer, he found himself performing various duties including aide to the cashier on a busy day.

Speaking about his growth, both professionally and personally, Benjamin said by September 1916 his salary had increased to 50 dollars a week. He then made up his mind and formally asked for Hazel's hand in marriage, which was given to him without hesitation. The engagement party was in November that was full of champagne and telegrams. However, one of these telegrams was not congratulatory; rather it was related to his draft status. He said this became a very troubling subject for him that he should put forward as clearly and honestly as possible.

Talking about the telegram regarding his draft status, Benjamin said in April 1917 America had declared war on Germany and an officer-candidate training camp was immediately set up in Plattsburgh, New York to prepare junior officers for the armies that would be soon formed. He decided to apply for the camp hoping to obtain the rank of Second Lieutenant. He armed himself with a formidable array of recommendations including letters from General Leonard Wood, Colonel Mitchum, the CO of the Governor's Island, and his old Dean Fredrick Keppel who was now Assistant Secretary to War. With this kind of support, Benjamin felt that he would enter the camp and hence much to the dismay of his mother and Hazel accordingly made his plans.

However, he soon received a stance note stating that according to the Army policy only US citizens could be accepted as officer candidates. He was disappointed because he was a British citizen as of that date and therefore they could not consider his application. They also returned his bundle of recommendations back to him.

Benjamin said this created a serious problem for him and his family. His two elder brothers were not earning much at that time and he was the major contributor to the family budget. He thought on the pay of the officer he could continue to look after his mother while it would have been difficult to do so with the personal allowance. He continued that the logical course of action was for his brothers to go into the Army when the time came and he would stay in the job claiming exemption from the draft as a support for his mother. He said he had reluctantly consented to that because he felt strongly about the spirit of patriotism that inspires youth to fight for their country.

Disappointed at one front, Benjamin then spoke about his wedding plans. He said he and Hazel had planned their June wedding for a long time. However, at the time of applying at the training camp, he had indicated to Hazel that the marriage might have to be postponed indefinitely. Nevertheless, when he was not accepted and it was also unlikely that he would be accepted later, they decided to go ahead with the marriage despite all the uncertainties. The marriage took place on June 3rd in the bride's apartment.

Benjamin's eldest brother Leon married his Nellie a few days before he was married. Nellie's family was very conservative and they felt that it was unfair for the younger brother to get a wife before the elder. Leon shortly joined the military and because of his years of training in the National Guards, he was sent to officers' boot camp. His lack of American citizenship was amended by making him a Second Lieutenant in the quarter master's corps.

Benjamin said around the end of 1917 he appeared before the Drafting Board regarding his application for exemption and that he was also expecting his first child at that time. The Board inquired about the circumstances of his marriage and Benjamin found himself in a humiliating position despite the courtesy that the Board members showed to him. They were struck by the amount of congratulatory messages at the time of his engagement last November. Mustering his courage, he said that family obligations prompted him to claim this shameful exemption and said that he however would accept the decision with some personal relief if the board ruled that he was subject to the earlier or later draft. Nevertheless he got the exemption.

Speaking about his regrets with regard to his army career, Benjamin said his failure to enlist in the real military and risk his neck along with millions of other youths remained a source of his regret and internal trouble for the rest of his life. He said even while speaking about this he can see a very unpleasant scene regarding his personal life before his eyes. He said sometimes in 1918 his mother moved out from her apartment to live with them, mainly due to financial problems, which he would discuss later. His wife Hazel never got along with his mother at all. His mother was a woman with complete independence, not being accountable to anyone. On the contrary, his wife was a spirited, conscientious and a dictatorial kind of woman. There was constant tension and a certain number of vocal differences between the two, with each seeking his support against the other. He added that during one such fight he remembers solemnly announcing his intention to leave and join the Army. Things immediately calmed down and his threat was soon forgotten.

Speaking about the political turmoil during those days, Benjamin said the year 1916 was the year of the Wilson-Hughes Presidential race, one of the closest in American political history. Wall Street was the centre of electoral betting those days. Almost everyone who traded in stocks called themselves 'speculators' (whereas today everyone is an 'investor'). He said those days they didn't make much distinction between their financial operations and racetrack or other bettings. He observed that readers may be surprised to learn that one of the services provided by the New York Stock Exchange House was to act as a stakeholder for the electoral bets of its clients. The fact that he was selected to take charge of the electoral betting department of Neuberger, Henderson & Loeb in 1916 would give some indication of the factual character of his activities with the firm, added Benjamin. He said almost all bets were placed on an equal amount and that he had a strong box full of cash and signed memos. There was great excitement the day after the election when no one knew who was going to win yet. In fact, on the third day, Wall Street officially announced Wilson's re-election and he was allowed to pay their fierce democratic speculators.

Coming back to his failures, Benjamin said that he would speak about his two serious failures in his financial career. He said his good friend Algernon Tesin, professor of English at Columbia College—an absolute bachelor and a frugal man—had amassed a substantial amount of savings. Most of his savings were invested in a very high-priced gilt-edged public-utility stock by the name 'American Light and Traction Common'. Benjamin said his early success with the Guggenheim Exploration liquidation gave him a keen interest in specialised operations such as arbitrages and hedges, as well as in the broader area of undervalued securities in which he put on stake as his own niche in Wall Street. He concluded that among other things he could make money conservatively and handsomely. It could be done by buying a common stock that analysis showed was under-priced and selling it against other common shares that the similar analysis showed as over-priced.

Benjamin said when he explained his views to Tesin and described some of the small successes he had achieved in this direction, Tesin showed great interest. They both set up an arrangement whereby they would supply a capital of 10,000 dollars in the form of twenty-five shares of American Lights and Traction and then sell them at about 400. Benjamin was to operate the account and the profits or losses were to be divided equally between the two.

Talking about the partnership, Benjamin said the account prospered significantly during the first year and he was able to withdraw several thousand dollars as his share of the profits. With that money he became the co-owner of the Broadway phonograph shop located on Broadway and 98th Street. His eldest brother Leon had long wanted to break out of the elite ranks of clerk of John Wannamaker. His interest in music and the phonograph had grown over the years. Leon learned from somewhere that a certain Mr. Irving Geon wanted to sell his Broadway business for a reasonable price. Leon found this as an excellent opportunity to fulfil his desire. Remembering their unfortunate venture into the moving picture business many years ago, Benjamin said he never had that kind of enthusiasm in that kind of business as his brother. Yet, he was happy to make it possible for his brother's dream to come true, he added. Benjamin said they paid 3500 dollars for the store's fixtures and goodwill and took the merchandise at wholesale price. The total investment was 7000 dollars. For the legal formalities, they called their family friend Alexander Rosenthal.

Benjamin continued that their phonograph venture was not a remarkable success. However, they carried on for several years before it was sold. As for the Aeolian record, he found himself in an ironic position—one that would occur several times in his career. The Aeolian Company had a palace on 42nd Street where they used to go in polite astonishment—either to ask for a favour or to defend themselves against their criticism that they were neglecting their product for the benefit of other labels. However, fifteen years later the Aeolian Company itself was in financial straits. Benjamin said that at that time his investment fund was the largest holder of Aeoline's guaranteed 7 per cent preferred stock and he became chairman of a protective committee to devise the best reallocation plant for their holdings. Benjamin said he was able to express some scathing words about the way Aeolian management was running the business—a role quite different from the ones he had played in the year 1917.

Benjamin said beyond ups and downs of Broadway and 98th Street, he was learning the hard ways about the pitfalls of Wall Street. Security prices declined steadily from the fall of 1916 till after the war ended in 1917. Benjamin said his operations of his old friend, Missouri, Kansas and Texas Railroad, which by his calculations should have been worth much more than their market value when the road was reorganised; however, its quotes along with their other stocks went down in general weakness. Speaking about the hardships at the stock market, Benjamin said the worst of all was that the bids started to disappear. The Tesin account called for a higher margin; however Benjamin was not able to replace the money he had taken out as it was all tied up in the phonographs, records and fixtures. Eventually it became necessary to sell some of the professor's beloved American Light and Traction stocks and that too at a considerable loss, yet, the account remained below margin and subsequently frozen. Benjamin said as far as the situation of his account was concerned, he had a loan in his account, which he could not repay. Still worse was that his management of Tesin's capital had been a complete failure.

Remembering the hardship he underwent during those days, Benjamin said he recalls one day spending lunch time wandering the financial district in a bleak gloom. At that moment he almost seriously thought of committing suicide. However, he returned to his old friend determined to tell the truth at once and to get the best out of his situation. The unambiguous Algernon was taken aback by his words. He, however, proved to be very understanding and sympathetic. Algernon suggested to him that he could make monthly payments into the account till his shortfall was covered. The amount was fixed at 60 dollars a month. Benjamin made these payments for about two years till the improvement in the general market and their own portfolios made further contributions unnecessary. He said, fortunately Tesin continued to have faith in him and in the following years he was able to increase Tesin's wealth to quite an honourable level.

Remembering some unfortunate events on his personal front, Benjamin said it was during this time of his financial crisis that his mother came to live with them and the quarrels between his mother and his wife Hazel had begun. However, soon his financial condition started to improve very fast and even before he was completely out of Tesin's debt, he was able to get a separate apartment for his mother. Benjamin said his mother maintained her secluded lifestyle for more than a quarter of a century, till her tragic death.

Speaking about his income post his earlier failure and some other disasters he had faced, Benjamin said his income mainly consisted of special operations of the arbitrage type and the usual sharing of the results of the Tesin account. Benjamin continued that he considered himself financially successful to quite an extent till the disastrous decline of the latter in the year 1918. He added, to some extent he had developed likings for the pleasures that the wealth he had accumulated could have made possible. In the year 1915 he also became a proud owner of an automobile in partnership with his cousin Lou which was the new 'Model A Ford', the successor to the Ford's ubiquitous and changeless 'Model T', he added. Speaking about his new toy like a child, he said in the early months of ownership of the car, people would gather in crowds around the car to admire its beauty filling the young driver with pride.

Excited about his new car, Benjamin said learning to drive in New York in 1915 was a different affair as compared to what it is today. Ford company used to offer free instructions to its buyers and hence he went to the sales office that was somewhere at Broadway and spent his 395 dollars for a shiny new touring car. He said he was then immediately taken to the West Road for his driving training. The first lesson was to learn how to crank the car, which was not easy for beginners, he added. He continued that after teaching the crank part, the salesman showed him how to more or less simultaneously deal with the three pedals (clutch, brake and emergency brake), the four positions of the gear shift, the spark advancer near the steering column and the retarder and hand throttle. Continuing his first encounter with the beast, Benjamin said he also had to be prepared to press the rubber bulb at the back to blow the small horn and every time he stopped the car on the first day of his learning, the salesman would ask him to get his feet off the pedals. He said, he kept trying repeatedly and at the end of a half hour training session the salesman said that he could drive now. Benjamin said he drove the salesman back to his sales room and then quite nervously drove the car down the dangerous road from the middle of Manhattan to his apartment in the Bronx. Anxious, he said he somehow managed to reach home safely.

Listening to what Benjamin said above, one would wonder about taking the exam for obtaining the driving license. Benjamin said in an amusing way that, "Believe it or not, in those days just owning the car was enough". He added, the law assumed that when one owns a car the person definitely would know how to drive it. Therefore, only non-owners needed a special driving license for which they had to undertake a test.

Jokingly Benjamin said that there was a saying in his family that he was a bad driver and had always been a bad driver. Blame was generously given to his emptiness rather than his lack of core competency. Nevertheless, in his defence he contended that in his 45 years of driving he had never caused even a minor injury to anyone and never damaged another person's car beyond a scratch. He further added that even his own car never suffered any damage other than a windshield incident, which had cost him a full 8 dollars to replace in those remote and happy days.

❑

Beginning of Actual Success

There were several ups and down in the life of Benjamin Graham. Yet, his upward progress on Wall Street was rapid, rather spectacular between 1919 and 1920. It was an encouraging period for him that was marked by his financial success, a steady increase in his standard of living, a broadening and deepening of his knowledge of life's material and intellectual pleasures, and of course, a tremendous sense of satisfaction that he felt about his position and esteem in the world. But as every good comes with bad and every happy moment is followed by a sad phase, Benjamin's life also saw some serious losses in the form of the death of his eldest son in 1927. Broken with the memory, Benjamin said it was a bitter blow, perhaps more startling because it came so suddenly in the midst of dazzling prosperity his family was witnessing. He continued that even his married life was not untouched by problems. Tensions were brewing which neither he nor his wife Hazel was insightful enough to identify and work in time. He was happily prepared to accept materialistic success as the goal and purpose of his life and forgot about idealistic achievements, he added.

Speaking about the success in his career, Benjamin said in the early 1920s he was made junior partner of the firm of Neuberger, Henderson and Loeb that was a member of the New York Stock Exchange. A fact, which was duly announced in the newspaper advertisements, he added. Benjamin said in this new system he was getting 21/2 per cent interest in the annual profit in addition to his usual salary that too without any liability for losses. He said over the course of four years his share of the profit was about 5000 dollars a year.

Further speaking about his success, Benjamin said it was in this year that he had his first experience with the Japanese Bond—a venture that earned him a special place on Wall Street. One of his friends, Lou Beroul, had given up his studies for a financial career and was working for Bonwright & Co., an important Bond House. The two used to go for lunch from time to time and on one such occasion Lou brought along a very young Japanese man named Junkichi Miki. A lively fellow that he was, Miki had come to America as a representative of a large Japanese Banking Firm, which had the idea of selling issues of American bonds in Japan, he added. Benjamin said Bonwright & Co. undertook to train him about the ways of American investment hoping to find an outlet in Japan for some of their own products.

Speaking about the turning events with Miki, Benjamin said the situation however developed in a completely different direction and Miki and his superiors soon learned that during the Russian-Japanese War of 1906, large profits could be made by buying various issues of Japanese government bonds held in different countries and reselling them to the investors in Japan. On one hand the appeal of these bonds to Japanese buyers was fuelled by post-war discrepancies in foreign exchange rates; and the right of investors to demand payments of a fixed amount in Japanese currency 'Yen' for principal and interest on the other, he added.

Following which the Japanese asked Bonwright to cooperate in obtaining and importing quantities of these bonds into Japan.

Unfortunately for Bonwright, the American firm was too busy with their own underwriting work and that they did not take much interest in the Japanese offer.

At lunch with Beroul and Miki, the young Japanese asked Benjamin if his firm had the European contacts and other facilities to do this reacquisition business on a large scale. Speaking about the offer, Benjamin said fortunately he was able to say that they could provide the Japanese with the comprehensive and energetic service they were looking for. Benjamin added that after they had completed a trial order or two to his satisfaction, Miki was up for a bigger deal. He agreed to engage their services especially for large-scale purchases and they agreed to buy only for Fujimoto Bill Brokers Bank of Osaka. He said that the bonds were to be sent to Japan with drafts attached and they were to get 2 per cent commission on every purchase. From this 2 per cent they also paid all expenses including cable and shipping charges.

Speaking intently about this new venture, Benjamin said that the business went into millions. They had established excellent contacts with brokerage firms in London, Paris and Amsterdam who were the original distribution centres of the Bonds. Due to the discount of the 'Franc' against the 'Yen', the Bonds in Paris were sold at a premium above their par value, as well as being able to be bought at a large discount by the Japanese investors even after incurring large brokerage expenses, he added.

Benjamin said he and Miki soon became good friends. From time to time Miki visited his house to enjoy their Jewish food. As a gesture of thanks for the Jewish food, Miki took him to a sumptuous dinner at the Nippon Club near Columbia University where Benjamin got his first taste of Japanese food. He said that he was in awe when he found himself swallowing various kinds of raw fish dipped in an assortment of sauces. However, sitting on the floor for two hours at a stretch proved an uncomfortable experience for him.

Further speaking about his friendship with Miki, Benjamin said periodically Miki introduced him to many Japanese VIPs, most of whom were from the financial world. One day Miki asked Benjamin if he could bring his friend Mr. Kwagai for lunch. Benjamin said that Mr. Kwagai proved to be an attractive, agile, friendly young man. During the meal they talked about Wall Street and several other topics.

Speaking of a blunder that happened during the meal, Benjamin said as they started to leave, Miki said with his unfailing smile that, “Mr. Graham, maybe you would like to see Mr. Kwagai play at Forest Hills someday next week? If so, then I would be happy to get you a ticket”. It was then that he realised that he happened to have lunch with a famous tennis player who had a good chance of winning the US Singles Championship and they didn’t say a word about tennis, his favourite sport, he added. Benjamin pondered on how stupid or unfortunate a man could be!

Further speaking about his friendship with Miki and association with the Japanese Stock Exchange, Benjamin said after a span of 35 years he went to Japan and there he renewed his friendship with Miki. After returning from there, he became an official of the Osaka Stock Exchange and then Professor of Finance at Kobe University. Miki took him to the Osaka Exchange and introduced him to the officials there. A surprise was waiting for Benjamin ahead when Miki also took him to the Director’s room where several people were seated. After introducing him to everyone in the room, Miki said politely, “And now, Mr. Graham, would you please give this meeting a 40-minute talk on the principles of security analysis?” Miki further added that, “He would be happy to translate whatever he would say”, said Benjamin. Benjamin said that this sudden happening had definitely exceeded his expectations. However, he did his best under those circumstances. He said at the end of every sentence Miki was translating his highly technical language into Japanese without hesitation and the people sitting in the room were nodding their heads in understanding.

Speaking about his time with Miki, Benjamin said that this renewal of friendship with Miki was very gratifying. He said Miki took him to the best Osaka restaurant and introduced him to the wonderful organisation called Geisha Girl. This time Miki remembered to make the eating experience more comfortable for his American friends, and therefore a well-like hole was dug under the table so that his friends from the West could sit comfortably without folding their legs. The Geisha were dressed in an aristocratic and lavish manner, were highly adept at song and dance and at Tamisen, and were constantly paying attention to their guests during long meals, observed Benjamin.

Back to the year 1920: Coming back to the year 1920 when he had met Miki in New York, Benjamin recalled that one evening Miki came to their house and asked how to play poker. He instructed him according to Hoyle and Miki carefully wrote down the value of various hands in a small notebook. After a few rounds of the game, during which he compared his hands with his notes, he declared that he was satisfied with his training and was now ready to play with his friends.

The incident was soon forgotten. However, a few days later when Benjamin met Miki, again, he asked how his game with his friends was progressing.

Aghast with the experience, Miki said, "Ah! Mr. Graham, you are a very imperfect instructor for the game. I lost a lot of money in the game".

Surprised with the technique that he used to teach Miki, which as per his knowledge was absolutely correct, Benjamin asked him, "Oh God! What went wrong?" Miki replied that Benjamin did not tell him anything wrong, he just forgot to tell him about bluff. Miki told Benjamin that his friends bluffed him all night and teased him when the game was over. Benjamin felt so ashamed of his unforgivable blunder that he even offered to make up for his loss. However, with true Japanese dignity, Miki declined his offer.

Further speaking about the friendship and financial gains in his life, Benjamin said that one of the most important and beneficial friendships of his life developed quite unexpectedly out of his analytical circles. He said, he was working on a detailed comparison of two railroads—the Chicago-Milwaukee Ad-St. Paul Railroad and the St. Louis and South-Western Railroad in 1919. In their trade, the railway routes were known by special names. He found out about this when he had just started working with the firm he heard one of their senior order clerks Murphy saying something like 'short stop'. Benjamin thought Murphy was speaking about 'short stock' and kept wondering why anyone would buy a hundred shares of 'short stock'. However, he was in fact referring to the St. Louis and South-Western Railroad that had the ticker-tape abbreviation of 'SS'. As for Chicago, Milwaukee and St. Paul was concerned it was usually referred to as 'Milwaukee', he said. However, that was not the case with Stock Exchange where the nicknames were based on ticker abbreviations.

Benjamin further said that his comparative analysis of the Milwaukee and SS quite convincingly showed that the SS Common and Preferred were a more attractive buy than the Milwaukee's similarly priced issues. In fact, Milwaukee appeared in an extremely unfavourable light, he added. Benjamin thought that it would be both fair and prudent to present his findings to the company official before publishing the circular. Benjamin said he went to see Mr. Robert J. Mairony who was Milwaukee's Vice-President of finance. His office was at 42 Broadway. Benjamin found Mairony surprisingly young for a Railroad Vice-President—a diminutive, Irishman with a lively wit. Benjamin embarrassingly told him about the purpose of his visit. Mairony went through his material quickly and handed it back to Benjamin saying that he had not found anything to argue in his facts or conclusions. Mairony said, "I wish we could do better, but it doesn't and that's it". Then Mairony asked him some general questions regarding work and soon they were discussing mediation that had become his forte and of which Mairony was also well aware. Mairony listened to him carefully and ordered Benjamin to buy 1000 shares for him. This was the lowest possible outcome of his visit to the Chicago, Milwaukee and St. Paul's office, adds Benjamin.

Speaking about his meeting with Bob Mairony, Benjamin said that strange incident was the beginning of a business and personal association between the two that lasted to the present day (June 1960). Bob Mairony became an investor in the Benjamin Graham joint account and then became a major stockholder and director of the Graham-Newman Corporation from its inception till it was liquidated. He also became a member of various protective committees and finally a director of the spectacularly successful Government Employees Insurance Group (GEICO) with him. They had been close friends through prosperous and difficult times and once it happened that Mairony also gave him a share of the profit on a successful deal because Mairony felt that Benjamin needed money to get out of personal financial difficulties.

Further speaking about his friendship with Mairony and the tragedies that struck his life, Benjamin said a few years ago Mairony, his wife Beatrice and daughter Marjorie were his guests at a yacht named Reposo that belonged to one of Benjamin's friends Dr. Herman Baruch, who lent it to him. Benjamin said, shortly after that pleasant trip, Bob and Bea lost their only daughter under extremely tragic circumstances. The incident was followed by another tragic incident when young Mairony had a stroke in their office a few years ago and had still not regained full control on his speech.

Benjamin continued and said that he had also made a literary effort on behalf of NH&L, which was a series of three short pamphlets entitled "Lessons for Investors". He said at the arrogant age of 25 he didn't realise the ostentatiousness of that title, nor his own arrogance in instructing an investing public that was, on an average, twice his age. Nevertheless, he thought, there was some wisdom in whatever he had said and that he was particularly proud of his strong argument for purchasing good common shares at fair prices. The root of this was the then-revolutionary statement that said, "If a common stock is a good investment, it is also an attractive speculation". This was because it gives the investor full value for his money. He added that if the market value of that stock is significantly lower than its intrinsic value then it should also have excellent potential for price appreciation.

Explaining the nature of his work, Benjamin said that his stint as a security analyst was not a major part of his job as a junior partner. Apart from this, he handled all the operations of the firm. He was an expert, and also attended to over-the-counter trading. He was also responsible for ensuring the efficiency of the office system and of course, he had a growing variety of clients who paid a substantial commission to the firm.

He continued that the US tax laws and regulations became complex as well as difficult post World War I. Benjamin studied the topic thoroughly because of its impact on the earnings of the corporations he was analysing. The fact that he knew more than the other people soon made him an expert and he earned a nominal fee by creating a return for many of his clients.

Benjamin said in 1919 they enjoyed a typical Bull Market marked by senseless manipulation on the part of insiders and a general combination of greed, ignorance and childish enthusiasm on the part of the public. He said about fifteen years later, during his period of playwriting, he decided to write a play about Wall Street. The glorious and tragic events of the years from 1919 to 1921 were then fresh in his mind. However, he rejected that period as he found them too strict to meet the standards of art. Rather, he returned to his memories of the years 1919 to 1921 and he included many of the characters he had seen in his boardroom, such as Riddle, the monomaniacal chemist whose only interest was American Coad Products stocks. He came to their office first to buy the most conservative Bonds available, then for careful investment in some of the 'best stocks', however, finally ended up losing his business and everything else because of ill-advised speculations.

Benjamin said, of course he cast himself as the protagonist in the play—an intelligent young man who profited from someone else's manipulation without any financial risk. He expressed this theme through a story about the transformation of a few small Pittsburgh companies into a huge transcontinental oil companies. He titled the play "Angry Flood". The play was never produced and he has no idea where the script is at present. He said the script undoubtedly deserves its oblivion.

Benjamin continued that in fact he came out very successfully from the dangerous period of 1917 to 1921 having learned a lot from his bad experience from the Tesin account in 1917. He said he did not let the extreme boom get the better of him and almost all his trades later were arbitrage and hedging, which gave him limited but satisfactory profits and kept him from serious losses.

Benjamin observes that it is not an understatement to say that he had become a smart cookie in his particular field. Yet, he was capable of doing some silly things in other areas of Wall Street, which he actually did.

Speaking about the inside working of the Stock Exchange, Benjamin said clearly Wall Street was a far different place in 1919 than it is at present. In those days it reflected the widest imaginable spectrum of morality. The members of the Stock Exchange and the Stock Exchange itself behaved impeccably among themselves. It was also highly reliable in the execution of orders of its clients and handling of deposited cash and assets. However, there were many of them who participated in blatant manipulation too. They would encourage investors to speculate, knowing absolutely well that almost all of them would end up with huge losses. They did virtually nothing to save the public from blatant cheating and manipulation.

❑

The Great Bull Market of 1920: He Was Almost A Millionaire

Benjamin Graham's journey has been quite colourful from several perspectives. It is the story that teaches many lessons and gives an insight of a man's ambitions and aspirations. Benjamin himself co-relates his school and career journey of inspiration and aspiration, saying that when he was in school he worked on various part-time jobs in many fields; however his career on Wall Street consisted only of two main jobs—first as an employee and then as a junior partner in brokerage; and second as the head of his own business. As he puts it, before going into his own business, he was seriously tempted by the idea of leaving his brokerage work to become a financial writer for 'The Magazine of Wall Street'. He said writing was his initial love and this was an opportunity to combine literature with finance. However, when he announced his temporary decision to his partners at NH&L, they succeeded in separating him from it.

Speaking about his family life, Benjamin said after the birth of their eldest daughter, Marjorie Evelyn in 1920 they decided it was time for them to try suburban living. Hence, they came to the top of the two-storeyed house in Mount Vernon, which was half a block from the Mount Vernon Country Club where Benjamin soon joined as a tennis member. They made several new friends there and joined an exclusive group of Jewish residents of Mount Vernon. Speaking about a couple in this group—Aaron, Gertrude and Hurwitz, Benjamin said Hurwitz was the classmate of Fred Greenman at Harvard. He had studied law there but never practised. Instead he became the right-hand man of Lou Harris, another of his classmates who ran a highly successful Harris Raincoat Company with his brothers.

Hurwitz learned a great deal about Benjamin's financial ideas and the particular ways in which he operated. The Harris brothers made an important offer to Benjamin—they said that he had to quit NH&L to operate a large account for them on salary and profit-sharing basis. They were willing to invest 2.50 lakh dollars with the promise of unlimited additional funds if the quality of his work and results were good. Also, as part of the original capital he was allowed to bring in his other accounts. He would receive a salary of 10 thousand dollars per annum and capital would be paid back at 6 per cent following which he would be entitled to one-fifth of the remaining profits—all on a cumulative basis. This proposal was worked out between them as early as at the beginning of 1923.

Remembering his past experiences with his firm about relieving him, Benjamin guessed that his firm would not let him go easily. However, this time luck favoured him. As a result of margin trading, the Stock Exchange had tightened its rules regarding the amount of free capital required for a one-member firm in respect of outstanding dues of its clients. The trade was expanding so rapidly that NH&L was unable to save the capital for arbitrage operation that Benjamin was running with such success. Therefore, the firm was reluctantly forced to refuse some of his good offers. They understood that his special talents lay in that area and that it was unfair to ask Benjamin to be in a company where his best activities would be strictly limited. Hence, the firm relieved him of his obligations more easily than he had expected. However, there was a catch. They asked him to do all or nearly all his business through them and in return they would allow Benjamin to use a rent-free office, a private stock ticker as well as various other services to operate his business.

The delight of his new found freedom, Benjamin started his own business that was incorporated under the name 'Graham Corporation'. To save a portion of his corporate income tax, they issued Participating Bonds to represent the entire capital, excluding shares of common stock, for voting and other purposes.

Benjamin said his old work ended and the new one started on July 1, 1923—nine years after he began his journey at 12 dollars per week with NH&L. He said he made this change without any regrets. He had long felt that he was not cut out for the brokerage business, which infuriated him from inside. This was mainly because he felt that the brokerage business could only prosper at the cost of the loss of its customers.

Further speaking about Graham Corporation, Benjamin said the company operated for two and a half years till the end of 1925 when it was dissolved. He said it was a successful venture, returning a high percentage on capital. He had limited his investments to his standard arbitrage and hedging operations and to securities that he found to be low in value. Benjamin said the first thing that he did in his new business was to buy some Stocks of DuPont and sell several times more shares with General Motors than that. He said at that time, DuPont Common was not selling GM's holdings for more than the value of its holdings, hence the market was virtually placing no value on its entire chemical business and assets. He said, because of this DuPont was grossly undervalued as compared to the market value of General Motors. With time, however, a spread-out appeared to be in their favour and he cancelled the operation at the expected profit.

Speaking about the rise of the Great Bull Market, Benjamin said that in the year 1925 the Market was well underway and more and more people were coming to the market. He said that this was a period in which most account managers operated discretionary accounts for their clients giving them the right to buy and sell whatever they liked without specific authorisation or orders. Several of these accounts were operated on a half-half basis, with profits being split equally between the client and his or her account manager. The best part was that in case of net loss, the account manager did not have to contribute any share. Benjamin said he had many friends at Wall Street who told him that he was foolish to work only for 20 per cent of the profits. His friends told him that they would bring him all the money he could handle—with a 50 per cent cut (part of which would be assigned to them).

Hearing all those friends, Benjamin began to feel that may be Harris was taking undue advantage of him. At 31 years of age, he was convinced that he knew everything, or at least as much as he needed to know to make money in Stocks and Bonds, that he was extremely successful on Wall Street, that his future was as limitless as his ambitions, that he was destined to enjoy immeasurable wealth and all the material comforts that money could buy. Benjamin said he started thinking about owning a yacht, a villa in Newport, race horses—may be even mistresses. However, he was still too naïve to include them in his list. He was too young to even realise that he was being presumptuous.

Drawn by his presumptuousness, Benjamin said in the middle of 1925, he made a new proposal to Lou Harris. He said that he would give up his annual salary, but instead after the allowed 6 per cent on the capital, he wanted 20 per cent of the first 20 per cent earned, 30 per cent of the next 30 per cent earned and 50 per cent of all the earnings over 50 per cent. To him this seemed like a logical enough arrangement.

However, Lou Harris was horrified at the idea itself that Benjamin wanted half of any profit at all, even if it was earned on

50 per cent of the capital. They agreed to end their arrangement fairly quickly and dissolve the corporation at the end of the year. Benjamin said if the Harris brothers had tried to reach a compromise, he was sure he would have agreed because he was never a stubborn type about specific demands. Nevertheless, he later found that they already wanted to separate from him even though he had done such a good job for them.

The reason, Benjamin said, was that after two years in close contact with his operations, with full details of the profit and loss of each buy and sell, Lou Harris thought he was now equipped with the brains and expertise to act alone. Why give Benjamin 20 per cent or more of the profit when they themselves can do better? Hence, Benjamin made his arrangement for the year 1926 and the Harris brothers made theirs and since they were both satisfied with the change, they parted ways as good friends.

Benjamin realises that before writing off the Graham Corporation affair, he must mention an associated account titled 'Cohen and Graham'. The Cohen of this partnership, he said, was a pale, short-sighted lawyer of about 35 years of age who was also a Harvard classmate of close friend Harris and Hurwitz. Cohen had some capital, maybe 1 million dollars and Lou Harris very kindly made a special arrangement for him, separate from, but similar to, the Graham Corporation. This venture also proved successful, though also terminated at the end of the year 1925. Benjamin said the reason he mentioned this insignificant account because Cohen of this Cohen and Graham was none other than Benjamin V. Cohen, who was later destined to join the famous team of Corcoran and Cohen with Tommy Corcoran, the architect of much important New Deal legislation and sometime assistant to President Roosevelt in pushing legislations through uncooperative Congress.

On January 1st, 1926 Benjamin transferred his services and funds to the 'Benjamin Graham Joint Account'. Most of the capital was contributed by his old friends including Fred Greenman, Bob Mairony and Heyman. The financial arrangement, he said, was exactly the same that he had proposed to the Harris group—

no salary, but a sliding scale of profit-sharing up to 50 per cent. The shareholders were to receive a quarterly payment at the rate of 5 per cent per annum against their capital or profits.

Speaking about the Benjamin Graham Joint Account, he said the account started with 4 million dollars and their capital after three years was about 25 million dollars. Most of its growth came from profits. Benjamin said a large part of this was his in the form of earnings on his growing capital, in addition to reinvesting his substantial compensation. Every year new friends were eager to deposit money in the account, he added. Benjamin said the popularity of the account was spreading and he made no effort to attract additional investment. In fact, he refused to accept money from people personally known to him, yet the number of his acquaintances kept growing.

Benjamin said the original group included one Douglas Newman – his classmate from Boys High School and Columbia College and a successful lawyer. A few years ago he had introduced Benjamin to his younger brother, Jerome, who was three years their junior at the same high school and later also went to Columbia College and then Law School. Jerome had married Reece, daughter of a rich cotton merchandiser and mill owner. Jerome, instead of practicing law entered his father-in-law's business and soon became second to him. Benjamin said he handled some investments for Reece and Jerry Newman.

Speaking about yet another transforming phase of his business career, Benjamin said in late 1926 Jerry came to see him and said that he wanted to leave Reece's business and join him. He was willing to work for Benjamin without pay until he proves himself valuable. Benjamin said this was the beginning of an association that lasted through the rest of his professional life, ending with his retirement in California and the dissolution of two businesses—Graham-Newman Corporation and Newman and Graham, which were formed after the 'Benjamin Graham Joint Account'.

❑

The Northern Pipeline Contest

Success is not for anyone to have forever. It comes and goes and sometimes even if it sticks for some period, it is in its nature to wander. Benjamin had also had his times of success and adversity. He ventured into several projects, some of which proved very fruitful and some painful. Speaking about some of his successful and unsuccessful ventures, Benjamin said that of the many deals made by the account, two were particularly memorable to him. The first included Standard Oil Pipeline Companies; whereas the second was Unexcelled Manufacturing Company, America's largest manufacturers of firecrackers. He said the first deal brought great success and the second great trouble without any ultimate benefit.

Benjamin explained that when the Standard Oil monopoly was broken up by the orders of the American Supreme Court in the year 1911, eight of the 31 companies that emerged from the giant consortium were small companies operating pipelines carrying crude oil from various fields to refineries. Very little was known about the finance of these companies. He further said that these companies only published a one-line 'income account' containing the net profit for the year and a balance sheet in as concise a form as possible. Only two Wall Street houses in the market were experts in all these Standard Oil subsidiaries. They published a monthly bulletin containing news items and statistics about each assistant. However, they never provided any data about the pipeline companies' finance. Rather, they only reproduced their grossly inadequate income and balance sheets.

Benjamin continued that one day he was going through the annual report of the Interstate Commerce Commission to get some detailed statistics about railroad companies. Surprisingly, at the end of the report he found some data from pipeline companies which, according to the table in the report, had been 'submitted to the commission for their annual reports'. He thought that such reports might contain information that was not provided to the stockholders and that might be interesting and valuable. Smitten by curiosity, he wrote to the ICC asking if they could send him a blank copy of the report to be filed by the pipeline companies. Soon, he received a heavy envelope containing a report form of about 50 pages filled with tables covering every detail of their operations and financial status. Benjamin said he was particularly interested in a table in which the companies were required to list their investments at cost and market value. All the pipeline companies had listed several investments in their annual statements. However, since no details were provided about the investment, it was not possible to know what they contained.

Fuelled by what he had found in the envelope, Benjamin took the train to Washington the next day and reached ICC building. He entered the record room and asked for the annual reports of all the eight pipeline companies for the year 1925. They were duly brought to him and he realised that he had hit a jackpot. He was surprised to find that all the companies had a substantial amount of excellent railroad Bonds. He found that in some cases the value of those Bonds alone were more than the full value at which the pipeline shares were selling on the stock market! Furthermore, he found that pipeline companies were doing relatively small gross business with a large profit margin and that they had no inventory. Hence there was no need for those Bonds investments. He saw that there was the Northern Pipeline that was selling for only 65 dollars a share, paying a dividend of 6 dollars while keeping about 95 dollars cash assets for each share, which was almost all the company could distribute to its stockholders—without the slightest inconvenience to its operations! And here they used to talk about bargain security!

Elated with the findings, Benjamin produced copies of the ICC report for the past several years and returned to New York. There he focused on acquiring the shares of the Northern Pipeline as the company had the largest amount of Bond investments in relation to its own market value. He said, through careful but persistent buying he managed to acquire 2000 shares out of a total of small capitalisation of their 40,000 shares. With this, it made Benjamin the second largest stockholder on record after the Rockefeller Foundation that owned about 23 per cent of all these companies. He thought now was the time to persuade the Northern Pipeline management to do the right and obvious thing—to return a fair chunk of extraneous capital to the owners, the shareholders. In his naivety he thought it would be easy to accomplish this task.

Benjamin said he made an appointment with the Company's President, D.S. Bushnell to meet him in his office that was in the grand building of Standard Oil Company. This was his first time ever to visit this famous building. When he went to Bushnell's office, he saw two very similar older gentlemen waiting for him. One of them was the President Bushnell and the other was his brother and the Company's general counsel.

Suffused with his knowledge and observations, Benjamin presented his point of view to Bushnell. He pointed out that the Company was only doing a gross business of 3 million dollars and hence it was absurd for them to be carrying 3.6 million dollars in Bond investment that had nothing to do with their financial needs. He continued that clearly in the interests of the shareholders the wealth needs to be distributed to them where it could be in direct possession of its full value, rather than at less than half its value as it is currently being confused with other pipeline assets.

Hearing what Benjamin had to say, Bushnell immediately replied that it was not possible for them to do so. “Why?” Benjamin asked. Bushnell replied that since they had no surplus, they could not pay out more than they earned. In fact, he added, their distributions were already very generous. Benjamin tried to convince them with the figures. However, at the end of a very long discussion and many arguments, Bushnell said, “Look Mr. Graham, we have been very patient with you and have given you more time than we could have afforded. To run a pipeline business is a complex and specialised thing that you may know very little about. However, this is what we have done all our life. You must give us the credit of knowing what is best for the Company and its shareholders. If you do not accept our policies, may we suggest that you do what good investors do in such circumstances. They sell their shares”.

Benjamin said that this was the full story, with slight variations which he was to hear countless times throughout his remaining professional career.

Aghast with his failure to convince the Bushnell brothers, Benjamin said, before leaving their office, defeated and disheartened, he told the Bushnell brothers that he intended to come to the next annual meeting of the shareholders to present his views in an oral memorandum. The brothers looked at a loss at the suggestion. However they overcame their confusion and quickly replied in affirmation and said that he would be welcomed. With this, Benjamin bade his farewell to them and left the office.

The annual meeting was held in early January of 1927 in the Oil City, Pennsylvania. To get there, one had to take a train to Pittsburgh and from there one had to catch some local means of transport to Oil City. The Company had very few offices there but large enough to hold the meeting. Benjamin said the meeting was attended by five more employees besides him. He said he could not find any shareholder from outside the company. Meanwhile, the yes-people of Mr. Bushnell were looking at him as if he was an alien. Followed by some formalities, an employee read out a pre-written slip presenting the Annual Report for the year 1926 for approval and acceptance. Then another employee quickly seconded the motion. Benjamin said he got up and asked, "Please tell me, Mr. Speaker, where is the Annual Report?"

There was the moment of embarrassing silence.

The reply was, "We are sorry Mr. Graham, but the report will not be ready for another several weeks". To which he replied in astonishment that how was it possible to approve a report that was not ready and available at the meeting. Mr. Bushnell replied, "We have always handled the matter in this way. Those in favour say 'Yes'." Benjamin said all proxies voted in favour except him.

After some other formalities, the Chairman said that the adjournment motion was in order. Benjamin said, he rose again and said that he would like to read a memorandum for the record regarding the financial condition of the Company as was agreed by them in New York.

The Chairman asked, "Would you like to put your request as a proposal Mr. Graham?" He did the same and put his request as a proposal.

It was the worst thing he could have done, observed Benjamin. Soon after he put his proposal the Chairman asked, "Is there any support for this proposal?" There was a break that was followed by silence. Benjamin realised that he had not thought about it and had not brought anyone with him from New York.

The Chairman continued, "Sorry Mr. Graham I can't hear any support. The motion must fall".

Frustrated with the situation, Benjamin said, "But as you know, I have made the long trip here to put this memorandum on the record. You too had encouraged me to do so. Mr. Bushnell I think you should show me the courtesy and see that my proposal gets the support".

In response to his outburst, the Chairman said that he was very sorry that no one was prepared to support his motion. He said, "Do I hear an adjournment motion from the house?" and just like that the meeting was over in a moment.

Benjamin felt humiliated for being fooled and ashamed of his incompetence and angry at the way he was treated. Trying to control his emotions he told the Speaker later that he had made a great mistake by not allowing him to speak. Benjamin added that he sort of warned the Speaker that he would come back the following year with a support and much more.

Benjamin said he completely justified his threat. In fact, in what he took to be a dismal personal failure in January 1927, it turned out to be financially fortunate. This was because he now had a full year to plan the campaign and raise his financial stake. With the increased capital, he bought more shares of the Northern Pipeline. Benjamin said he took as much risk as he could with the partnership money. As counsel, he engaged the highly respected corporate law firm of Fred Greenman, Cook, Nathan and Lehman. Alfred A. Cook was the senior partner who had great ability and prominence. However he was equally pretentious and arrogant.

In January 1928, it was the day of the annual meeting. Benjamin said he went to the Oil City. However, this time he was not alone. He was accompanied by three attorneys from Cook's organisation including Alfred himself and Henry Schnauder who was their Pennsylvania attorney. They had a decent number of proxies this time that were enough to give them what they wanted.

The next morning, before the meeting started, the management called for a conference. Benjamin said they had proxies for over 15,000 shares that were enough to entitle them for two directors. President Bushnell was very polite to him this time. He said that he would be more than happy to accept the nominations of two directors on their behalf making the elections unanimous. Alfred Cook proposed Benjamin's and Schnauder's names as directors. Bushnell tried his level best to get Cook to give his own name or almost anyone else's name instead of Benjamin's. It was obvious that Bushnell didn't like him. Cook replied in categorical denial. He said this was Benjamin's fight and he deserved to win. Bushnell surrendered. The single slate was duly nominated and elected and the entire meeting went off quite smoothly.

Proud of his achievement, Benjamin said now he was the first person not directly associated with Standard Oil Company to be elected as a director of one of its subsidiaries. He said, although the Northern Pipeline was smaller than most, he was very proud of his exploits and achievements.

❑

Family and Other Issues

Benjamin was an astute businessman who took various risks in his professional career. A good student and curious young man, Benjamin was always experimenting with opportunities. So much so his family life was also a sort of roller-coaster with various ups and down. Benjamin married Hazel, who was initially his eldest brother Loen's love interest. Both Benjamin and Hazel were attracted to each other from the very first day they met and eventually got married in June 1917. Benjamin said his dear son, Isaac Newton, was born on May 1918. Then after a gap of two years Benjamin and Hazel had their first daughter, whom they named 'Marjorie Evelyn' for no particular reason and after a usual long discussion. Coincidentally, 1920 was the year of the song 'Marji' which was a very simple composition. However somehow it lasted for many years. Benjamin said their Marjorie instantly became 'Marji' for all of them. Exactly five years after the birth of Marjorie, they had their second daughter—a baby girl with blue eyes and blonde hair. They called her 'Ellen Dorothy'. The name Ellen was a romantic reminiscence of Tennyson's 'Idylls of the King' –

"Ellen the Fair, Ellen the Lovable, Ellen the Lily Made of Astolet".

Dorothy was his mother's name, informed Benjamin.

Speaking about his first son, Benjamin said that Newton was a wonderful boy right from his early infancy till his heart-breaking death shortly before his ninth birthday. Benjamin said undoubtedly the passing years have led him to exaggerate Newton's qualities, mainly because in reality it is not possible for a child to be as perfect as he was in his memory. He was very handsome, full of charm, highly intelligent, thoughtful and very friendly, added Benjamin.

Narrating the events of a trip he and his wife took with Newton, Benjamin said that he remembers when Newton was three years old. They took him to the New York Hippodrome – a spectacular palace with beautiful views, which is no longer in existence. It was famous for its huge water tank, which always held an important place in the entertainment at that place. At a certain time the tank would be opened, several mermaids would take their places and then gracefully dive into the water. The spectators watched them in curious silence. Suddenly a childish, but very clear voice was heard, "Mother, why are they taking a bath? Are they dirty?" That voice definitely belonged to their son, Newton.

Narrating another incident of his innocence and intelligence, Benjamin said once his grandmother Mazur came to live with them. She was made to sleep in Newton's room. Next morning they asked him about everything. He happily replied, "It was all right". However, Newton added, "But you know we snored so much that the palace shook". This phrase, which he had heard several times, describes the monster sleeping in the Jack and the Beanstalk. He was trying to spare his grandmother's feelings by saying 'we snorted', however, the way he presented his report made them all laugh.

Newton had to be admitted to the hospital due to his deteriorating condition. While talking about his final weeks at Mount Sinai Hospital, Benjamin said when they informed him about his sister Marjorie been awarded a Blue Ribbon for best work in her class, his face lit up. Newton said with a grave expression that, "You don't appreciate Marji enough. She really is very smart."

Speaking about the bond that Newton and Marjorie shared since the very beginning, Benjamin said, Newton and Marjorie knew each other better since childhood, better than his wife and he himself. He said, although Marjorie began speaking at a normal age, her speech was very slurred. In fact one can say that she had her own kind of speech. They had a hard time understanding what she was saying. However, Newton, who was constantly with her, never had any problem understanding what she had to say and could tell whatever she was saying without any difficulty. Therefore often when Marji tried to say something to them without success, they used to turn to her four-year-old brother to decipher what she wanted them to know. Newton would always tell them without hesitation what Marjorie wanted them to know.

Talking about Marjorie, Benjamin said initially her 'pie-face' seemed quite domestic. However, she soon turned into a very charming child and then a beautiful young woman. Her initial temperament was very different from her brother Newton, who was always sweet and polite. Marjorie had a different personality. She sometimes behaved in a rebellious and defiant manner, he added. When Marjorie was about three years old, they returned to New York from Mount Vernon. There the Grahams hired a governess for both Newton and Marjorie. The governess Luisa Gohel, also known by another name "Fräulein', was from Stuttgart and was thoroughly German in her mannerisms. Fräulein soon revealed that Newton was her favourite and did her best to discipline Marj. Obviously she was the wrong choice for their daughter, observed Benjnamin. However, they didn't realise it at first. For a while they thought Marj was a spoiled brat, who she probably was. However, luckily for her and her parents she grew up to be a perfect daughter, an excellent student and a great athlete, said Benjamin. He further said that since the age of thirteen, Marj had given him nothing but the feeling of joy and pride.

Marjorie was not only a bright child, she had a strong desire to excel and to do superbly in all her efforts. As a baby she had learned to stand on her head and would maintain that posture till they asked her to stop. Benjamin said he remembers on one such occasion when Marj was probably about six years old, a serious question came out of her mouth while she was doing her head stand. She asked, "Daddy, what is the world record for headstand?"

Speaking about her talents, Benjamin said Marjorie used use that stunt to her advantage when she was a member of the swimming team at Lincoln School by regularly taking first place in back-dives in the headstand position. She showed considerable aptitude for music, especially for original compositions, he added. Talking about her theatrical endeavour, Benjamin said Marjorie and two other talented students of Lincoln School wrote and produced a play called 'Seventeen Million Dead', in which they recounted the carnage of World War I and made an eloquent plea for peace.

Talking about his second daughter, Benjamin said Ellen was to achieve Graham Bell PhD and later wife of Cyril Sofer. Ellen was born in the year 1925. She was the wonderful combination of blue eyes, blonde hair, beautiful face and a charming demeanour. Benjamin said she was very dear to all of them including her brother and sister. Hazel often remarked that Ellen was the best-natured of all three of their children, added Benjamin. He further said that the children's governess Fräulein soon began to call her 'best' and the title was accepted by other children without complaint.

Talking about Ellen, Benjamin further said that she was about to develop a character of her own with some unexpected traits. She thought and acted for herself and sometimes erected an impenetrable wall between herself and everyone else. Her basic independence manifested itself at a very early age that too to the point where she even had an encounter with the police as a child.

Narrating the incident, Benjamin said that at the age of six Ellen decided that she wanted to hear the birds singing at Central Park and to do so she had to wake up early. One Sunday morning she woke up early in the morning; got ready and took Newton junior, her three-year-old younger brother and left the apartment at 6 am in the morning. Benjamin said they only found out about this when a police officer, who had found two young children wandering around in the park, woke them up. Benjamin said they do not remember if they had punished that sweet girl for her amateurishness.

Talking about their education, Benjamin said both Marj and Ellen had the privilege of studying at the 'Lincoln School'—an illustrious institution funded by the Rockefellers and run by Columbia University's Teachers College. Its purpose was to experiment with several promising ideas in primary and secondary education. It had teaching staff of the highest quality and carefully selected students. The school gave preference to the children of the Columbia faculty. Benjamin said their children had greatly benefited from the liberal and challenging environment at the Lincoln School.

Benjamin further continued that Ellen had given them many opportunities to be proud of her since a very young age. Before she was even nine years old, she appeared on the stage of both Town Hall and Carnegie Hall. The children attended the Diller-Quail School of Music that taught music in the latest ways. The students performed at the Town Hall every year. Children in first grade, who were about seven years old, usually appeared as a small percussion band with drums, triangles, cymbals among other things. However, after a trial, Ellen was chosen to lead the orchestra and she gave an extraordinary performance in an extremely subtle version of 'The Champbells Are Coming', beautifully controlling her entire group. Benjamin said he almost choked with emotions when he saw Ellen's performance and looked around to see if others were as thrilled as he was by this wonderful spectacle.

When Benjamin came back to New York from Vernon with his family, they first settled in an apartment at the ground floor of a house on 160 Riverside Drive at 88th Street. He said that at that time it seemed that their apartment was big and luxurious making him proud of his achievements as his Riverside Drive address signalled financial success. However, later in 1926 they moved to another rented house, which was a pleasant house near the casino, of which they also became members.

Speaking about his own extra-curricular activities, Benjamin said in New York he also joined a City Athletic Club. The club that time had one main rule—'No card games to be played anywhere within the club premises'. At CAC he learned two new sports—Squash and golf, he added. Benjamin said he also enjoyed skiing—a sport he started in the winter of 1924 at the Dean House on Lake Mahopac. There was plenty of snow and skis were available for guests who wanted to take a sporting risk. He continued that little Newton and he showed a natural skill for skiing. They had a rudimentary motion-picture camera gifted to them along with the projector and screen by his old firm NH&L on Christmas. The family archives still have the first reel made from that camera showing them having a blast on that first ski trip, he added.

Benjamin said the introduction to the Bell and Howell movie camera was more important for his wife Hazel than expected. She later took up photography as her career. For many years she was the official photographer of the enormous Hadassah organisation as well as a member of its national board. Her films on life and landscapes in Israel had been shown to appreciative audiences everywhere.

Benjamin said that some of the happiest and funniest times of his life were spent on skiing holidays. They often took the night train to Lake Placid for the Christmas holidays. Most of the skiing was done at the Stevens Hills near the hotels, where there was only one towrope. Benjamin said they once spent their Christmas vacation in Lake Placid with their good friends Charles Goodmans and his children. He said the eldest of his children was Robert, an attractive college student. Benjamin said he loved the way they sat till late at night talking about philosophy, reading poems and having a wonderful time. An incident from this holiday highlights the clash of temperaments between Hazel and him, added Benjamin. He said since they were to be at the hotel on New Year's eve, he decided to take his formal wear with him on the holidays. For some reason, Hazel was against attending the formal event and tried to stop him as well, he further added. Benjamin said he told Hazel that he had to go and because Goodmans was wearing formals, he also wanted to do the same. After all there was a grand New Year party at the hotel. Goodmans went on to get ready and so did Benjamin. He said in their room Hazel begged him not to wear evening wear as she would feel embarrassed if he wore his evening wear and she did not. He remained adamant, he added. Benjamin told Hazel that the entire thing was about her high-handedness. He said that she had no reason not to bring her evening dress with her. He was tired of always following what she said. Benjamin felt that it would be foolish on his part not to wear his formal clothes even after taking the trouble of carrying them there.

Benjamin continued that when their argument escalated, Hazel took his dress shirt that lay on the bed and threw it out of the window into the snow. He said, calmly he took out another dress shirt from the drawer and started putting studs on it. Enraged by his action, Hazel snatched the second shirt too from his hands and threw this one too out of the window. Benjamin said he had no choice but to surrender—angrily of course—and eventually he shuffled down the hall for dinner with embarrassment in an ordinary suit.

Remembering the incident at the hotel, Benjamin said no doubt a psychologist would draw several conclusions about the state of their marriage from that incident. Benjamin said that in his opinion both Hazel and he were decent people whose strengths outweighed their flaws. They had many wide ranging interests—mainly their children. However they were both interested in theatre, opera, concerts, travel, sports and charitable activities. He said it was Hazel who got him interested in working for the blind before they got married. She used to teach dance to the children at the Dyker Heights Home for the blind and later at the newly founded New York Guild for the blind Jewish people. Benjamin said he started as 'Big Brother' to a very handicapped blind boy all because of the interest Hazel had aroused in him. Later, he added, he was about to become the Chairman of a Director's Budget Committee and eventually the President of the Guild, whose annual budget grew from 30,000 dollars to the most recent 1.3 million dollars. This was one per cent increase over the United States' Gross National Product.

Opening about the flaws in his married life, Benjamin said they had more reasons to expect a happy and successful marriage than many couples. Why did their marriage fail, he wondered. A less important reason was, perhaps, a certain lack of physical compatibility, presumes Benjamin. He said the main difficulty, he believed, grew from a flaw in his character, which prevented him from taking Hazel's flaws head on in the way he should have. His wife's outstanding qualities were her energy and her various practical abilities. However, she had one drawback. She was sure that she could handle everything better than anyone else. She naturally took the lead in all practical arrangements. Because of all this, she had developed a habit of dominating the people around her including her husband, he added. Benjamin said he was not the kind of man who would tolerate such behaviour. Although, he added, he loved to oblige and hated to bicker about anything, he was completely independent and inwardly opposed to every form of domination.

Further speaking about the relations between his wife and himself, Benjamin said before Hazel or he could suspect that something was wrong with their marriage, it failed. He said in the summer of 1926, while living in a cosy vacation house, he used to play golf on Wednesdays at the swanky Deal Country Club with Bert Parker. Parker was the manager of the local office of McDonald and Company. Benjamin said life seemed comfortable, luxurious, interesting and rewarding in many areas at that time. He continued that during that weekend, his middle brother Victor came to visit them and commented that everything was going more than fine for Benjamin and his family. Benjamin agreed with his brother and then said, "Probably things are going far too well and possibly we might suffer some enormous grief in future." No wonder, he said, his comment turned out to be prophetic.

Explaining his agonising prophesy, Benjamin said in early March of the following year, they had just returned from a vacation in Florida when they learned that Newton was suffering from an ear infection. They called Dr. Freisner, a renowned ear specialist at Mount Sinai Hospital, who diagnosed Newton with Mastoiditis. The doctor said this required an operation. However, Benjamin said, after the operation Newton developed spinal meningitis and eventually died on April 20, 1927. Newton was about to turn nine on May 12 that year, he added.

Benjamin said Newton was buried in their plot at Westchester Hills Cemetery. The footnote of his grave is inscribed as – 'Most Loving, Most Bravest, Most Dearest Child'. Benjamin said he was all that and much more.

Speaking about life post Newton, Benjamin said he felt connected with Hazel in the times of their grief. However, that sense of connectedness indicated more clearly than they thought that they were pulling apart. Shortly after the funeral, they went to a Chinese restaurant for lunch. They talked about starting a new and better life together. He said, Hazel felt that she should share the things about her life with him that she had kept hidden.

Benjamin said he was a stoic, relatively disinterested husband—who was more immersed in his own career. Hazel was a person who needed more warmth and understanding and she found it in a friendship with their family doctor. Hazel told him that it was a close friendship and nothing more. Benjamin asked no questions and took her word for it and promised her to be a better husband in future. Hazel also promised him to change.

Soon they were longing for another child—dreaming of another Newton. They wished for the boy whom they had lost to be reborn. Benjamin said Hazel got pregnant in due time and believed resultantly everything should be fine between them. However, it didn't happen. A great deal of sadness and the best of intentions were also not enough to heal the deep-rooted conflicts between a husband and wife. They quickly went back to their old ways, he added. Benjamin said in fall, despite her pregnancy, Hazel announced her intentions to travel to Russia with a close friend, Pauline H. As anticipated, he was too busy to go along with her.

Hence, he was single for two long months, adds Benjamin and continued that it was then at the age of thirty-three and ten years of marital fidelity, he had his first extramarital affair. "The girl", he said. "Let's call her Jenny". She was about his age, not pretty, had a reputation for being outspoken and sharp, and, most strangely, had been their close friend for the past fifteen years.

Speaking about his "love life", Benjamin said their love affair was being carried on under many constraints. Leading among which was the fact that he was very busy. They could hardly see each other and meet only briefly. Benjamin said he had been faithful to Jenny in his own way for about seven years. Throughout this time, her behaviour towards him had been exemplary. She rarely pointed out any fault in him or demanded more than what he used to give her. However, in the year 1933 or 34, Jenny told him that their relationship was very unsatisfactory and that she was tired of living it that way. She decided to end it by spending some time in Mexico. Benjamin said they parted as good friends.

Coming back to his wife's pregnancy, Benjamin said their second Newton was born on April 10, 1928. His birth brought happiness both for Hazel and himself. This was like a special request to send a boy into their life.

The second Newton was a handsome boy with huge brown eyes and black curly hair. Benjamin said no child could have had received a more enthusiastic welcome and loving care than he did. However, Dr. Wilson, their family doctor for several years, had some troubling news. It seemed that there was something wrong with the child's thymus gland and there was a possibility of serious problems for him in the future. Benjamin said because of this apprehension, they took special care of the child.

Benjamin said he was telling this with a heavy heart that after the first few years their second son was going to give them less happiness and more worries and sorrows. He didn't really seem comfortable with them. It was very difficult to understand him and soon it became clear that he was highly neurotic and in all likelihood schizophrenic too. Sometimes they blamed themselves, Benjamin added, because they named him after their first son Newton and believed from the very beginning that their first son had returned to them.

Benjamin said several questions arose with regard to second Newton that—Did he get confused because of that name with regard to his identity? Was he offended at being compared with the incomparable lost paragon of their family? Had his special physical care weakened his character? Benjamin observed that he was sure that there was no substance in these speculations and it was only Newton's and their misfortune that he was born that way.

Benjamin said with all that was going on in his life, he wanted an extra occupation for his mental energies as well as a distraction for his misery. Some time ago he was thinking of writing a textbook on security analysis. He decided that before presenting his views in printed form he should first prepare a college course on the subject. Furthering his decision, Benjamin contacted Professor James Egbert who was head of Columbia's extension department and expressed his views. Professor Egbert liked his idea and scheduled a course on 'Security Analysis' for the fall of 1927. Everyone was surprised at the response it got and the course was highly successful with over 150 registrations.

With this launch Benjamin's academic career took off which was to last for more than 40 years. This included professorships with various degrees at Columbia and UCLA and lectureships at other institutions.

Benjamin said in the fall of 1928 the Ben Graham family was ready to take another step to do something really splendid this time. Benjamin said, huge office buildings and equally impressive apartment houses were being built in all of New York's better districts. They heard that the old Beresford Hotel at 81st and Central Park West, where one of their closest friends Greenman had lived for some years after his marriage, was to be replaced by a thirty-storeyed apartment building of ultimate luxury. This was what the very ambitious Grahams wanted. From the offered plans, they selected duplex apartments with a terrace on the 81st and 19th floors. It had ten rooms and God knows how many bathrooms. Servants' rooms were also available near the terrace. The rent was to be 11,000 dollars a year and the lease was to last for 10 years.

Benjamin said they were not at all apprehensive about taking on such a huge responsibility. These were much smaller than the figures he was used to. For the year ending they had to show about 60 per cent return on their 1.5 million dollar start-up capital. His own profit before taxes exceeded 6 million dollars. He did this by following extremely conservative methods—keeping his risk of loss to a minimum compared overzealous speculation in overvalued securities around him. Benjamin was amused at how wonderfully gifted he was. This was before the catastrophe happened! The last thing he did that year was to sign a 10-year lease for their Beresford apartment, which was due to expire in the fall of 1929. They signed the lease in their drawing room on a train that was taking them to Palm Beach for their Christmas holidays.

❑

Mid-Point of Life: Beginning of Cataclysm

Nel mezzo del cammin di nostra vita
Mi ritrovai per una selva oscura
Ché la diritta via era smarrita
(Midway along the road of our life,
I found myself in a darkened wood,
Where the true path had been obscured)

This is the beginning of the great poem of *Dante Alighieri* that he wrote in the year 1300 at the age of 35 years. Dante's life's journey was actually more than half way through, for he died in his early fifties as did his idol Virgil and the great Caesars, Shakespeare, Molière, Beethoven, Napoleon and many others. Benjamin said in the year 1929 he too turned 35 years, the age at which his father had died. However, he stated these words in the summer of 1964 so that this chapter represented a middle point for him in a very real sense. Benjamin said it would be an exaggeration to suggest that like Dante, he was about to have a full taste of hell. Yet, there were occasions when he felt he was falling into an abyss of trouble and despair, which was unfortunate because those were the exact opposite of his days of glorious success.

In fact, the first half of the year 1929 brought exciting and commendable events for Benjamin. So much so that the terrible aftershocks that followed caused comparatively less harm to him. Benjamin said his massive troubles were to come in the next three years. Nevertheless, in its implications the year 1929 was as fatal to him as it was to others.

Speaking about the changes in the stock market during 1929, Benjamin said various types of investment trusts were being formed during this period. The former were fixed trusts, fairly innocent in character, in which a bank held a specified portfolio of common shares as a trustee and each stockholder had a pro-rata share in that irrevocable portfolio. Then the management trusts arrived—companies whose executives could modify the portfolio just as they were doing in the Graham Joint Account. There was nothing inherently wrong with such an arrangement. In fact, it had proved itself quite successful in England for several decades. Although, like any financial institution, this too needed honest direction and sound policy. However, the speculative climate of the late 1920s had seduced or corrupted almost all the important people in finance and the hitherto unquestionably honest firms were driven towards questionable activities.

Benjamin said in the meantime, Bernard Baruch unexpectedly came into his life. He added that about a year ago he had the privilege of meeting the great man and he suggested several Graham type investments to him. All these investment ideas appealed to his deep sense of security values. These included issues such as Plymouth Cordage, which was sold at around 70 dollars and paid a handsome dividend and had over 100 dollars per share in working capital alone. Others were the Pepperell Manufacturing Company, a household name in bed sheets and pillow cases, and Haywood and Wakefield, a leading manufacturer of baby carriages. All these shares were selling well below floor price by the normal standards of private business and were ridiculously low compared to the prices of the most popular stocks of the time. These anomalies reflected the bizarrely unfair character of the stock market in the late 1920s.

Benjamin recounted that Mr. Baruch was gracious enough to listen to his analysis, accepted his selections and purchased substantial quantities of each share. He added that of course from his point of view his consent was sufficient reward for his labour and to some extent he was right too, because just the knowledge that Mr. Baruch supported his decision and that they now had common financial interests was valuable enough to him. Benjamin said that on two occasions Mr. Baruch had to make efforts to secure his election to the boards of companies in which they both owned the stock. He succeeded in one such effort. Benjamin said, however, Mr. Baruch had not taken this step to help him. Rather, he did this to improve his own investments. Benjamin observed that in various contacts with that eminent person during his career, he had never seen Mr. Baruch doing anything helpful or generous for him as an individual or for that matter for anyone else in his knowledge. Benjamin continued that Mr. Baruch had arrogance that diminishes the greatness of some, and probably it might be Mr. Baruch's vanity, rather than true generosity, that encouraged him to give large sums to charity and other causes for which he had made huge contributions. Mr. Baruch had received extensive recognition and praise for his charity works that he had always desired.

Further speaking about Mr. Baruch, Benjamin said once he got a message from him that he would like to meet Benjamin in his office. When Benjamin reached his office, his secretary, Miss Boyle informed him that Mr. Baruch was busy and asked Benjamin to wait. The wait went on for half an hour after which Mr. Baruch came out of his office. To his surprise, Mr. Baruch was taking his afternoon nap during this half hour. Benjamin thought Miss Boyle should have told him about his arrival.

Nevertheless, when they went inside Mr. Baruch's enormous office, he told Benjamin that he was going to make an offer to him that he had never made to anyone else before. Mr. Baruch wanted him to be his financial partner.

Explaining his offer, Mr. Baruch said, "I am 57 now and it's time that I slow down and let a young man like you share my burden and my profit". He further said that for this purpose Benjamin had to quit his current business and devote himself entirely to this new partnership.

Benjamin, surprised by the offer, replied that he was very pleased, rather astonished by his proposal. However, he felt that he could not abruptly end and close the highly satisfying relationship he had with his friends and clients and for reasons that would be explained later, ended the matter then and there. He, however, contemplated the scenario for the next seven years that might have been much better, if only he had accepted Mr. Baruch's offer on his conditions without giving much thought about others.

Speaking about his Joint Investment Fund, Benjamin said negotiations with the Heintz partners for the purpose dragged on for months. In the meantime in August the first serious fall in the market happened and they decided to shelve the project for the time being. However, the Joint Investment Fund project never happened. The terrible crash of early September 1929 dropped the stock averages to half in a matter of days. The prospect of the Graham-Heintz Investment Fund vanished into thin air and he and Neuman turned their attention back to the Benjamin Graham Joint Account. There was much to think about, he added.

Benjamin said after the massive fall of September 1929, they covered many of their short positions and made lucrative profits. However, in most cases they didn't sell the preferred shares as their profits were too low. They ended the year with a loss of only 20 per cent compared to DJIA's massive loss. Many of their participants had their own margin accounts that suffered enormous losses due to the pyramiding effect of the borrowed money. Almost everyone was pleased with the results of the accounts for the year, he added. In fact, he had heard himself referred to as a 'financial genius' more than once mainly because he didn't lose much. The year 1929 ended in a period of some price recovery and relative peace. Benjamin said most of them believed that the worst was over.

Speaking about their Beresford Apartment, Benjamin said there was still some time for it to get completed. Therefore they could not move into their regal duplex till October 1929, the time when the Wall Street deluge was at its height. Benjamin said he was never really happy in that palace. As soon as that became a reality, he regretted the 11,000 dollar rent and 10-year lease contract. Besides, he added, the whole place seemed colossal. There were endless decisions to be made about furnishings and décor. This left him in a quandary. On one hand he had no real interest in such matters and therefore even shopping for the same was a tedious task for him. On the other hand, if he had left all the decisions to his wife Hazel, it would have confirmed her belief that she was the boss of the family by right of superior knowledge on every subject, added Benjamin. He said currently he does not remember how he solved this dilemma. However, he remembers that they had spent a massive amount of money on the décor.

For the winter months of 1930, Hazel had rented an apartment in St. Petersburg, Florida where she was to go with the children and Benjamin was to go on a long vacation. Benjamin said his stay in Florida in January was marked by an incident that made little impression on him at that time. However he would remember it often later on.

Speaking about the vacation, Benjamin said his wife Hazel met a man named John Dicks who was a 90-year-old man. His father had founded the John Dicks Uniform Company of Long Branch, New Jersy that Benjamin had often passed this massive factory on his way to deals. He went to see Mr. Dicks at his residence in St. Petersburg and found the old man surprisingly alert for his age. Mr. Dicks asked him everything about his business. The number of clients he had, the money he owed to the banks and brokers and a myriad other questions. Benjamin said he answered every question politely but with confidence. Suddenly John Dicks declared with great seriousness, “Mr. Graham I want you to do something that is very important to you. Take a train to New York tomorrow, go to your office, sell your securities, pay off your debts and return your capital to your partners. If I were in your position right now, I would not be able to sleep a second at night, and you shouldn’t sleep either. I am older than you and more experienced than you, so you should take my advice”.

Listening to the old man, Benjamin got up and thanked him for his advice. He said that he would consider his suggestion and soon pushed him out of his mind. Benjamin thought that Dicks was not far from his hallucinations. Perhaps he could not understand his mode of operations and his ideas were absurd. However, it just so happened that he turned out to be 100 per cent right and Benjamin 100 per cent wrong. Benjamin said he often wondered what his life would have been if he had taken his advice. He was sure that would have lessened his worries and regrets. However, would his character and future career have been shaped the way it was shaped after his ordeal? This was another question to ponder, observes Benjamin.

The downfall of the Stock Market had affected a great deal of people during that time. However, Benjamin said, the early 1930s marked a good recovery in the Stock Market from the previous year’s decline. He said by April the DJIA had reached 279, which was an increase of about 41 per cent from its low of 198 on November 13, 1929. However, soon the overall economic picture turned bleak due to the credit failure and a second major decline occurred, which was to continue with relatively few interruptions, till the DJIA hit a low of 42 in June 1932, he added.

Benjamin said despite an encouraging start, the year 1930 was to be the worst in his 33-year history of managing finances. He said their loss for the year 1930 was a whopping 50.5 per cent. Nevertheless in the successive years the loss decreased as in the year 1931 it was 16 per cent and only 3 per cent in the year 1932 - which was the comparative victory. Yet, the cumulative loss for the years from 1929 to 1932—before the tide turned its course - was 70 per cent of their proud capital of 2.5 million dollars in January 1929.

Benjamin said they, however, stubbornly continued to make quarterly distributions of 11.25 per cent, which went out of his and Jerry's capital, leaving the balance of only 22 per cent of the principal amount by the end of 1932. Various participants of their Joint Account withdrew all or part of their capital. One of them was Bob Mairony, who apologetically explained that he needed his money to fulfil his other obligations. Benjamin said they gave Mairony a proportionate share of the issues from their portfolio, which was a minor debt at that time.

Recalling that tough period of his financial uncertainty, Benjamin confessed that only one person made a new investment in their fund during those difficult years. It was Jerry Newman's father-in-law Ilias Reece, who invested 50,000 dollars at almost the lowest point of their business. This meant that with his characteristic shrewdness, Ilias Reece was to receive a very high reward for expressing his faith in them. Benjamin said he was forever grateful to Reece for his help at that crucial point.

Benjamin continued that they worked very hard to recover their finances over the years and managed to make various beneficial arrangements affecting their holdings.

Clearly his family needed to cut down on their lifestyle expenses tremendously, said Benjamin, especially as the account under the indemnity contract was not paying him any salary, just 1 per cent of the earnings to run the business. The main problem, he added, was to get rid of the humongous lease at Beresford.

Fortunately they were able to sublet the apartment to one Mrs. Marcus of Neiman-Marcus, a Dallas department store, for about a year, he added. They later got out of the balance of the lease by paying some compensation, and moved into another affordable, but quite impressive apartment at the El Dorado on 91st Street and West of Central Park.

Speaking about the downslide of the stock market during 1929, Benjamin said everyone had read about the doomed speculators who were said to have jumped from the windows of brokers during the market panic of 1929. Those stories were greatly exaggerated to appeal to the masses, he added. However, Benjamin said, it was true that many people in those terrible times acted out of desperation, generally because they believed themselves to be doomed due to the market crash, although the fact was they were not doomed to that extreme extent. Citing an example of his first mistress's uncle, Benjamin said he made a fortune in the shoes business and then moved into real estate. However, he was worried about various kinds of losses and decided to opt for an easier solution to his troubles. He locked himself in his garage with a bottle of whisky and the car's running engine. Benjamin said, the fact was he was quite solvent and left his family in a comfortable position as his investments in their funds; his wealth had subsequently turned into millions of dollars.

Confessing his own similar feelings of doom and gloom, Benjamin said he sympathised with his old friend's desperation and almost with his sad end as he had also suffered similar feelings of despondency for more than three years. He said that it was true that he was not completely ruined; however he was at his lowest point of finances, which probably ten years ago would have seemed enormous. He continued that both 'wealth' and 'poverty' are relative terms—a poor man in New York would be considered a rich man in Calcutta; and that every person who had lost nearly a fifth of his wealth would feel that he had suffered a calamity, no matter how much he was left with. Benjamin revealed that the main burden on his mind was not the actual shrinkage of his property, so much as the long struggle, post tide, repeated foreclosures and the uncertainty that whether or not the depression and losses would ever end. He continued that even the realisation that he was also responsible for the wealth of many of his relatives and friends who were as apprehensive and distraught as he was with regard to their future finances. He said that hardly anyone can better understand the sense of defeat and despair that gripped him and almost dominated him till the very end.

He further revealed that the decline confirmed the thrifty attitudes and habits that the tight financial conditions of his early youth had inculcated in him. However, he had almost completely overcome in years of his success. He said he did not blame himself so much for his failure to save himself from the disaster he himself was predicting, but for slipping into an extravagant lifestyle for which he neither had the temperament nor the capacity to take pleasure in. Benjamin said he quickly convinced himself that the real key to material happiness was a moderate standard of living, which could be achieved with little difficulty under almost all economic conditions. He said he applied this new theory in two ways—one logical and reliable enough, the other quite conservative.

Benjamin further confessed that he became determined to never again indulge in appearances, unnecessary luxuries, or expenses that he simply could not handle. He said the Beresford lease was a bitter but salutary lesson and for the next 35 years he avoided all kinds of white elephants of real estate. However, he continued, on yet another ground of purely personal spending, he admitted that he took economy too far and started worrying about dimes and quarters once again, whereas in reality thousands of dollars were at stake. He said he used to take the subway instead of taxis convincing himself that it was faster and that he was always in a hurry. However, he knew it well that he wanted to save the dollars the taxi ride would cost him. Benjamin said he hated to admit that he even started to order less expensive dishes on the menu for himself, while on the other hand he took his mother to expensive Chinese restaurants for their weekly dinners. He further admits that in his days of prosperity he had provided his mother with a car and a driver (though, he had never hired a driver for himself). However, now he felt that during his need of strict finances, his mother would understand the requirement and could do without them. Fortunately, he said, he almost always had made a big difference between the spending habits that others indulge in and those affected him. He said, he was pretty sure that he was never misunderstood to be stingy, though it would have been so if the world knew how he treated himself.

Benjamin said during the difficult times of 1931 to 1932 he was engaged in many activities. He wrote articles for *Forbes* magazine, pointing out the extraordinary discrepancies between the low prices of important common stocks and the huge amount of assets behind each stock. One of the articles he wrote titled, "Is American Business More Dead Than Alive?" This was the question that was to occupy an important place in future financial terminology. Benjamin said he participated in many economic discussions and a wide variety of groups. He continued to give his course in Colombia too, though in very small classes. However, apart from all that, in 1932 he began to work with certainty on the textbook that he had first introduced during his prosperous times in 1927.

Working on his decision to go ahead with the project, Benjamin said he asked Dave Dodd to collaborate with him on the book. They both decided that Benjamin would be the senior author and write the entire text in his own style, whereas Dave would assist with suggestions and criticism, check various facts and references, and prepare the tables. They prepared a table of contents and a sample first chapter and submitted it to McGraw-Hill through Huge Kelly, who was a bright young employee and their former student. McGraw sent their material to its reader, a professor of finance at Harvard. As an exception to the rule, they were shown the professor's report, which was very favourable. The only doubt the professor had was whether they would have the strength to carry the ambitious task to a conclusion. McGraw-Hill was so impressed with the recommendation that they offered them a straight 15 per cent royalty instead of sliding scale starting at 10 per cent. He and Dodd agreed to split the royalty in the ratio of 3/5 for Benjamin and 2/5 for Dodd. The contract was signed in late 1932; however it took a year and a half for the first version of *Security Analysis* to come out.

Further revealing his ventures in this field, Benjamin said in December 1932 before the fall was over, he began two entirely new activities that were to play a vital role in his later life. One was as an expert witness in valuation matters and the other was his invention of the Commodity Reserve Currency Plan. This invention was to find him a place in many economic textbooks in the future. Benjamin said he would discuss these later when he would describe the next period of his life that began in March 1933 with the inauguration of Franklin D. Roosevelt.

❑

The Road Back, 1933-1940

Benjamin mentioned various stages of the Stock Market that showed downward and upward trends over 1929 to 1932. There was a complete crash and some recovery in the Stock Market and then there were also setbacks for various operations in the Stock business. He said the year 1932 brought some relief for the Stock Market and the investors. Yet, DJIA bottomed at 42 in 1932, which was still better than the previous couple of years and it ended at 59. However, it again fell at 53 with President-elect Roosevelt closing banks, though it again began its upward climb, ending the year 1933 at 99. Yet, it showed no net change in the year 1934, though again it climbed to 144 in late 1935, he added. DJIA reached the Bull Market top at 197 in March 1937 making their operations successful once again, said Benjamin. He continued that, in fact, they outperformed the market by a lot that year. He said, they began the year 1933 with a capital of 375,000 dollars, which was far less than their figure of 250,000 dollars four years earlier. However, in 1933 alone their profit was better than 50 per cent. Benjamin confesses that with this encouragement he felt a renewed confidence in his abilities that was also shared by their participants of the Joint Account. Most of these participants were their old personal friends and their companions during the unfortunate times.

Apart from his operations at the Stock Market, Benjamin said he was also expanding his services as a consultant. Mentioning an incident that opened a new phase in his career, Benjamin said the US Treasury Department had a lawsuit regarding property taxes owned on the controlling shares of Whitney Manufacturing Company that made chains. The Treasury wanted an expert witness to testify on the value of a stock that was not sold in any market. The people at Columbia School of Business recommended his name and he was hired. The executors of the estate claimed that the value of the shares should be determined by the very low level of Stock Market on the date of the owner's death in the year 1932, as well as the fact that the company—like most other companies—was losing money that year. Benjamin said that it was his belief that shares should be valued like a private business as they represent a controlling interest and the owner could do whatever he/she wanted with the company and its assets. He said, he concluded that if the business is being liquidated then the value of the controlling shares should be based on the value of the minimum business.

Benjamin said he believed that the reason a business should continue was its value as a running business rather than as a liquidated one. He estimated the liquidation value, without any discount for substantial plant investment, and thus the shares, at an amount equal to net working capital. These views were in line with his analysis and assessment of several articles that he wrote, notably in the year 1932 series in *Forbes* magazine.

Benjamin stated that the tax court found a value almost equal to the value he supported and much more than the estate claimed. This was his first case and his first 'victory' as an expert witness on valuation. This was followed by perhaps 40 more cases involving a wide variety of financial situations, he added.

Further speaking about his side businesses, he said he kept updating the *Security Analysis*. He continued to keep his views on investment in the second edition of 1939 conservative and monetary. The most recent revision, he added, the fourth edition that he wrote in 1962, proved to be the most difficult one and took a long time.

Confessing the 'crash' in his personal life, Benjamin said he underwent divorce with Hazel in the year 1938 and he then married Carol Wade. Carol was a beautiful woman; however living with her was a very difficult task. Finally they too got divorced in the year 1940. Benjamin said even though their relationship was stormy, he continued to socialise extensively. Giving an example, Benjamin said he was part of a group of security analysts who met at Helen Slade's apartment once a month to discuss business, drink heavily (all but him) and equally generously got to enjoy the famous buffet hosted by Helen and her husband Henry Sanders.

Speaking about Helen Slade, Benjamin said she knew almost everyone in the more intellectual areas of finance. A dozen prominent personalities were in regular contact with her. Some talked to her on a regular basis over the phone too. For years she was the driving force behind 'The Financial Analyst's Journal', he added.

Further speaking about Helen Slade, Benjamin comically mentioned that Helen was very fond of cats to the extent that her 'cat-love' exceeded boundaries that even Benjamin, who himself was a cat lover, found unthinkable. Alexander was Helen's favourite cat and she gifted the cat with gifts like—she bought a genuine pearl necklace that the cat wore around its neck publicly. Helen also purchased a significant number of shares and registered them in the cat's name. Describing an award that Helen named after Alexander after his death, Benjamin said, the 'Alexander Award' was established after the said demise of the feline that was given annually for the best article published in the 'Financial Analysts Journal'. However, after the death of

Helen Slade, the 'Alexander Award' was changed to another appropriate name as the 'Helen Slade Award', and later it was also named after Benjamin and his friend Dave as the 'Graham and Dodd Award'.

Admitting his own love for cats, Benjamin said he and his second wife Carol were also very fond of cats and that his attraction for the animal has always been irrational and Carol was not far behind. He further said that they together bought a baby Siamese who they named Sheharzade—'Sherry' in short. The feline turned out not only into a beautiful cat, but also was very affectionate and disciplined. He said their love for her was one of the few feelings that they shared and said that the first year of their marriage would have been an unmitigated disaster if it had not been for Sherry.

Remembering the time after his second divorce, Benjamin said after his divorce with Carol he spent most of his time with his mother and brothers. He said he was also busy in finalising the 1940 edition of *Security Analysis* with David Dodd.

Describing the state of foreign affairs at that time, Benjamin said his domestic difficulties went together with the dangerous mode in foreign affairs. Where on one hand he was dismayed by the rise of Hitler, on the other he was stunned by the surrender of Chamberlain in Munich. These developments were discussed in detail at the monthly meetings of a select group of financial analysts, of which he was also a part. When World War II broke out in September 1939, its effect on the Stock Market was the exact opposite of the shock of World War I. Benjamin said the prices of commodities immediately skyrocketed. However, there was very little fighting in the first months of the conflict and only a few people were killed, he added. Benjamin further revealed that the American public grew tired of what was often referred to as the 'phony war'.

Benjamin said the horror of World War II soon started to raise its head when in May-June 1940 came the massive and lightning-fast German offensive, which was soon followed by the fall of France and the miraculous yet hopeless escape of British forces at Dunkirk. Benjamin said, it was at this time that he found himself really moved by the situation. He became restless and depressed and even less able to cope with his domestic issues. He said it was at this point that he pursued his childhood sport—roller-skating again—something that he had rarely done since he was a child. Describing his experience with the skating at that point, Benjamin said the constant whirling, the rhythmic body movement, the soothing music and the roar of hundreds of turning wheels used to bring a strange kind of comfort to him. He would start the session with sad thoughts about the state of the world and bitterness towards Carol; however, in the end would find himself thinking only of the tricks of skating. This would bring a welcome sense of calm upon his soul, he added.

❑

His 'Career' As A Playwright

It is well known by now that Benjamin was a man of various talents. A financial expert, an analyst, a lecturer and of course a writer. One of his multi-faceted talents was a playwright. He himself confessed that he had written several plays, however hardly any one of them saw the light of stage. As he himself puts it, during the period of his most intense professional activities, he somehow managed and found the time and energy to write a few plays. One of them saw the light of production in two different stages, he added. He further revealed that the origins of his first play was somewhat strange as while going through some old papers in the year 1930 he found a cardboard box on a shelf in their apartment in Beresford. He casually opened it and found several letters written by a married artist to his wife Hazel. Some of them were quite objectionable, even if they were trimmed. He said by that time his relationship with his wife Hazel had become quite strained.

Benjamin said those letters could have been of great strategic importance to him at that time if he had wanted to use them at the time of their divorce. However, he only did that once in a very private way between his attorney and the attorney of his wife Hazel at the end of their marriage.

Benjamin confessed that he kept two letters out of them all and didn't tell Hazel that he had seen those letters. Strangely enough, despite all the contacts they had over the next 35 years, he never spoke to her about them. It is just at this time he revealed the information. However, this incident gave him the idea for a play, on which he soon started working.

Benjamin said he named his play 'China Wedding', referring to the twentieth year of the marriage of the main characters. His characters were the perfect couple. The husband is a highly successful lawyer, the wife a beautiful woman active in many noble causes. There is a French artist in the story with whom the female protagonist of the play had a love affair a few years ago. The reason she gives for the love affair was that because her husband was an intellectual and logical man and refuses to give himself completely to his wife. However, later the love between the wife and the artist turned into friendship and their romance ended.

Further speaking about the play, Benjamin said that the wife kept Raoul's (the artist) powerful letters with her. The letters were addressed to a private box at the post office. However, they were inadvertently left in a folder on her husband's desk two days before the play opens. The crucial question is whether the husband has found and read those letters or not. The husband never mentions them in the play. However, the wife understands that it would be in his character to know the secrets and not say anything about them. Benjamin said it was for the viewers to decide that whether the husband knew about the letters or not. He said there are also some supporting characters in the play, particularly an eighteen year-old daughter and her fiancé. There is also a strange incident in the play wherein the lawyer gives unorthodox advice to his daughter's fiancé about sex.

Benjamin said he asked his wife Hazel to read the script and give her views. She returned it saying that she liked the play very much. However there was not a single word about the subject matter nor was there any hint of surprise or bewilderment that he might have discovered her secret.

Benjamin said during that time they were friends with Sylvia Golden, the editor of *Theatre* magazine and John Golden's sister and was also a producer. Sylvia liked the play and thought that the great David Belasco might produce it. Benjamin said he sent the play to him and after a while he was sitting in David's office for an interview. David certainly spoke very kindly to Benjamin. However, what was even more certain was that he rejected the play.

Benjamin said later the play was accepted by a leading firm of theatrical agents, Young and Rubsman. However this was the only approval the play received.

Continuing his artistic streak, Benjamin said he had other thoughts and plots for other plays in his head. He said he came up with a script for a Vaudeville Sketch and wrote the dialogue in just one sitting. The name of the play was—'The Day of Reckoning', he added. The play begins with the scene of a barber's shop. The backdrop of the play is that years ago, the barber's wife was seduced by a sly friend who also siphoned off her savings. Now, in the scene, a bearded customer enters the shop and asks the barber to groom him. Soon the barber recognises the man as the cause of their misfortune. The play ends with the villain dying of horror under the dangerous razor, narrates Benjamin.

Benjamin said he gave the play along with 'China Wedding' to Harry Dalph, an old friend of Hazel. Harry had made a profitable career in Vaudeville along with his sister Juliette. Though Harry's speciality was dancing, he had also been a successful playwright too. Harry told him that his play was good; however, the story was quite similar to that of 'The Emperor's Barber'. Furthermore, since Vaudeville had sunk too low there was no room for anyone to produce new sketches in that market. Benjamin said this was the end of 'The Day of Reckoning'.

Benjamin said soon after his script was rejected, Harry Dalph asked him for a proposal. He had a wonderful plot for a three-act comedy play. Harry was impressed with Benjamin's dialogue writing skills a thought they could collaborate on the box office 'knockout'. However, there was one small complication, he added, which actually proved to be an advantage for him. Harry suffered from Buerger's disease, known in the media as the horrifying name of 'thromboangiitis obliterans' that had affected his legs to an extent that he had to give up his performing career. Benjamin said Harry had the foresight to protect himself by taking adequate insurance policies through which he used to receive a handsome amount every month under the 'disability' clause. However, he added, such payments would stop if Harry became self-supporting once again. Therefore, insurance companies were keeping a close watch on his activities. Under these circumstances, Harry felt that it would be dangerous for him to be known as the co-writer of a new play. Hence, their joint work would have to appear under Benjamin's name only. Yet, they could share the huge profits equally and the film rights could make a major contribution to it.

Benjamin said it all sounded great to him at that time and he accepted Harry's offer without giving much thought to it. However, he added, when he sees it in retrospect, this was far from credible action on his part as he was helping a beneficiary in taking advantage of some insurance companies, or rather 'cheating' them.

Benjamin said Harry Delph's idea was for a highly influential editorial writer whose tentative title was 'True to the Marines', which was clearly inspired by Arthur Brisban, who was the great connoisseur of the Hearst newspapers at that time. Benjamin said he started working on the play in the summer of 1933. He remembers that clearly because he used to visit Harry's house by the sea once a week for long discussions. Eventually Harry was satisfied with the work and took on the task of producing it. Benjamin said a stock company that performed at a Red Barn Theatre in Locust Valley, Long Islands, agreed to try out the play for a week or two to start their season. Both Benjamin and Harry received a nominal amount for their permission. The first show was played in June 1934 – about the same time when 'Security Analysis' hit the market. The play was 'reasonably successful', he added.

Speaking about sudden changes in his finances and life that brought both happiness and a feeling of pride, Benjamin said the 'coming out' of his first book and the production of his first play happened almost simultaneously. This gave him a feeling of great satisfaction, which was bordering on pride. He was excited by the excellent returns offered by the Joint Account, which promised to put a definite end to his own financial woes and his worries towards his clients. In addition, he said, he was increasingly in demand as an expert witness, a profitable secondary occupation for him. Benjamin said at this stage he was 40 years old, yet a French writer described him as 'the adolescence of old age'.

❑

Commodity Reserve Currency Scheme

Benjamin Graham's name has been associated with several finance related aspects of the early 1900s. However, the Commodity Reserve Currency Scheme was considered as one of his major achievements. Benjamin himself said that if there is any chance that his name would be remembered by the future generations, it would be as the inventor of the Commodity Reserve Currency Scheme. He further explains that to describe this plan he had to begin with a disclaimer about the subject matter. He said his formal study of economics was limited to four weeks in the year 1912 at Columbia College under Dr. Mujje as he had to give up many of his courses to take a day job at the US Express Company. Economy was one of those subjects that he had to drop, he added. Benjamin said when he returned to the College the following February, he could not fit economics into his schedule and he dropped it without giving a second thought. Despite this meagre training in the 'dismal science', Benjamin established himself as an authority in the theory and practice of Security Investment, in Corporate Finance and, indeed, in Economics. He said that he learned everything about economics the same way as he learned about finance—by reading, thinking and by hands-on experience.

Benjamin said his economic invention has found its way into most standard works on monetary theory. The great Lord Keynes wrote an article about Benjamin's idea. Benjamin said that the letter Lord Keynes wrote to him on this subject would form part of his collected works when it would be published.

Explaining the concept of the Commodity Reserve Currency Scheme, Benjamin said the idea of a commodity-based reserve currency, or CRC as he would refer to it as, first occurred to him in the depression of 1921-22, when the world was perhaps faced with poverty in the midst of abundance. Raw materials were generally produced in excess as compared to effective or cash demand. Commodity prices fell catastrophically, causing all kinds of financial distress, which led to the increase in the vicious cycle of unemployment and economic crisis. Benjamin said from the beginning of his study of that distress along with pervasive pain as its attendant, he felt that it was all basically unnecessary and that the repetition should stop. If a nation lacks the means of production—fertile land, manufacturing capacity, and technical know-how—it must have a lower standard of living. However, it seems logically absurd for a country like theirs', which has so many resources, to find itself unable to buy its own products and suffering from overstocking of goods in warehouses, whereby there is shortage on the shelves of its families, observes Benjamin.

Further speaking about the decline in the economy, Benjamin said in seeking a solution to this vexing problem, he first considered the situation of gold producers. They were free from the hardships that plagued the rest of the world. No matter how large their production was, they could sell their commodity immediately for a fixed price—which was 20 dollars an ounce at that time, he added. Benjamin further analysed low wages and low prices reduced their cost of production and increased their profits, benefiting them largely in the market. Benjamin said that many economists suggested a plan to stabilise the general level of prices; however, none found any widespread acceptance. Benjamin observed that the best compensation at this time was Irving Fisher's proposal for the dollar, whereby the amount of gold equivalent of a paper dollar had to be increased or decreased to offset a rise or fall in the price-levels. Benjamin said his own reflection on the problem suggested to him a completely different solution, a better standard. The basic, he realised, was to give a monetary status to a specified bundle of raw materials or 'market basket', which was always given to the gold. This meant that the owners (producers) of the whole set of commodities could always exchange then in their proper relative proportion for a fixed amount of paper dollars in the treasury, while holders of paper dollars could always exchange them for the same number of baskets, he added.

Benjamin continued that in his view, there were both active and passive interests in the commodity-reserve proposal. On the active side, it tackled the problem of stabilising the price-level as directly as possible by defining the dollar in terms of commodities and establishing two-way convertibility between the paper dollar and its defined commodity equivalent. In a broader sense it would create a bridge between the world of commodities and the world of money – allowing commodity units to move and function as money as needed and money back into the world of commodities and consumption. Benjamin said the idea is reminiscent of the famous story of the seven fat and seven thin years in the 'Bible' and Joseph's wisdom in storing up the surplus against the later need.

Benjamin continued that on the passive side, it did not attempt to stabilise the price of a single commodity, as unsuccessfully attempted by so-called price-fixing schemes in the past. However, he added, his plan allowed each commodity to fluctuate in price according to changes in its supply and demand conditions—while maintaining stability against the bundle of commodities as a whole.

With every new experiment come various problems too. Benjamin said the difficulties of putting this theoretically appealing idea into practice were obviously enormous. Should dress manufacturers and countless similar businesses be made capable to sell all that they pay to the US Treasury for a fixed price? Apparently not. There are many things like quality, legality, reasonable price, brittleness, obsolescence, and above all assuming the government was getting money to pay for all this. What would it do with these products?

Benjamin confessed that the idea had hit him during the depression of 1921-22. However, he only discussed it with his uncle Maurice Gerard at that time who liked it immensely. Yet, he kept the plan aside during the next boom years when he was too busy making money on Wall Street.

Benjamin said he published his plan after 10 years. They were in the midst of the greatest depression in their history—all the paradoxical distortions of 1921-22 were now being repeated; however, to an extreme extent. One of its results was intellectual excitement, marked by the formation of many discussion groups, diverse proposed remedies, and the launch of various movements to bring about radical changes in the economy. Chief among these was the radical takeover idea, known as technocracy. The second was, Benjamin added, Upton Sinclair's 'bootstrap project' in California that was known as 'EPIC'. The third was the famous Townsend Plan, which advanced the then-revolutionary proposal of a pension of 60 dollars per month for people over the age of 60 years.

Benjamin further added that an economic interest group was formed and met regularly at the New School for Social Research in New York City under the sponsorship of the school's distinguished president, Dr. Alvin Johnson. Benjamin said he immediately joined the group that was named 'The Economic Forum'. The aim of the group was to exchange ideas on how to improve the 'situation out of order'. In a session in the year 1932, Benjamin presented his plan. In fact, he presented four different plans that he had dreamed up. The first was the Commodity Reserve Currency Scheme, largely in its final form, but without the figures and calculations that were to be added in the plan. The second was that there was an idea for large-scale slum clearance and its replacement by less expensive housing - with subsidies for former slum tenants to the extent necessary to meet the new rents. The third was a scheme under which people who had lost their jobs were entitled to personal loans based on their skills and experience, which were to be given to them by the Federal Government in the form of unsecured loans at low or no interest and which would allow them to pay their loan after they found jobs on reasonable terms.

Mentioning his fourth proposal, Benjamin suggested that France could replay the principal and interest on its net debt. He proposed with some sense of humour that they send 40 million bottles of wine, including champagne to America every year, and that every American citizen of voting age get a free bottle for Christmas. The allocation of liquor was to be done by lot, seniority or any other equitable method, he added.

Speaking about the economic group that he was part of, Benjamin said two members of their group boldly decided to publish a journal, using their excellent name—The Economic Forum—to publish new proposals deemed worthy of attention by the editors. The senior editor was a young man named Joseph Mead. Benjamin said he knew nothing about Mead's career ahead of that time. The second editor and publisher, he added, was even younger, although already a member of the New York Stock Exchange, a bastion of conservatism. However, he was open to new economic ideas, in which he was deeply interested. His name was William McChesney Martin. Benjamin continued that little did they know that their Will Martin was destined to be elected the youngest Chairman of the Exchange in history and would go on to become the head of the US Federal Reserve System, thereby becoming one of the most powerful financial influences in the world.

The Editors of their forum—Mead and Martin asked the members to submit articles for their magazine. Benjamin said he wrote his Commodity Reserve Currency Scheme under the title 'Stabilised Reflection'. The article was published in the second issue of 'Economic Forum' in the year 1933. This was the first official presentation of the CRC to the public, he added.

Speaking about his invention, Commodity Reserve Currency Scheme, Benjamin said in the three decades since he had invented the scheme, this original idea had given him both satisfaction and frustration. A psychological situation was created at the very beginning, he said. Benjamin further added that there was a brief moment of great excitement at the beginning of 1933 when he learned that his lawyer friend David Podell had managed to generate interest of his classmate, President-elect Franklin D. Roosevelt in the idea, and that it was under serious study in Washington as part of the anti-depression programme. Benjamin said something in the inauguration speech of the new President which led him to think that the President was in favour of the CRC idea. Naturally, he added, he was over the moon. Benjamin confessed that he had envisioned himself as the well-known and respected saviour of America's and perhaps the world's economy. However, nothing happened after that speech. Though, about two years later an important member of the Department of Agriculture, Lewis Bean, a noted statistician and advisor to Secretary of Agriculture Henry Wallace, came to visit him.

Bean told Benjamin that Roosevelt had formed the Commodity Credit Corporation to support the prices of agricultural products and was purchasing large quantities of agricultural goods. Bean saw in his plan a way to finance those goods by issuing money directly against them, with an increase in money in circulation stimulating the general price structure, he added. Benjamin said Bean gave him a lot of personal encouragement regarding his idea and provided some useful data on prices for the book that he eventually wrote on the subject. However, no official action was taken by the Agricultural Department on the subject.

Further speaking about the CRC plan, Benjamin said clearly the CRC was seen as a very radical innovation in Washington. This was, of course, being opposed by Bean's partner and rival Mordecal Ezekiel, who had other economic plans under his sleeves. Therefore, once again nothing happened on this front. Benjamin added that as far as he knew, Bean had never publicly supported the CRC plan, perhaps because it would have been undemocratic on his part to do so. However, he gave Benjamin various moral exhortations periodically and also sent him some historical data that he was allowed to include in his book.

Once again disappointed by the bureaucracy, Benjamin said in the year 1937 he worked in a book-form presentation of his idea for the CRC. The book came out in the year 1937 with the title *Storage and Stability*. Benjamin added that while choosing the title of his book he had the alliterative title 'Progress and Poverty' by Henry George in his mind. He said he had dreamed that one day his book *Storage and Stability* would take a place in economic literature at par with George's masterpiece. He admitted that he had worked very hard on the book and the facts and references from other authors are supported by the many notes that appeared in the book's appendix. The book also included various calculations involving price variations in the offered commodity unit. These were made by his young niece, Dr. Judith Poole—an expert in Haematology. Benjamin said he first asked McMillian to publish the book, who very politely declined the proposal. And, although McGraw-Hill had reasonable scepticism about the book's commercial prospects, yet he agreed to publish it—probably out of respect for the success of *Security Analysis*, he added. However, Benjamin said, this was on the condition that Benjamin would take the unsold copies of the first edition as a guarantee against the loss. Benjamin confessed that this was not an honourable arrangement, yet in his eagerness to get the book published, he accepted the offer. How many authors have felt compelled to do so for works that they thought would be a milestone in the history of thought, he observed.

Benjamin said several academic economists supported his plan and persuaded him to launch a publicity campaign to present it to the general public. They needed someone to act as the executive director of the committee for this purpose. Benjamin said he found one Norman Lombard for this job. However, he does not remember how Norman used to make his living, he however remembers that Norman was married to a school teacher, which undoubtedly helped a lot. He was associated with Irving Fisher in the stablecoin consortium and later ran some regular monthly economic discussions. They also included the Committee for Economic Stability which Benjamin was heading as a Chairman. Benjamin added that they sent out literature and membership forms and managed to get 50 or so professors of economics to become members of the Committee, including many notable names. However, despite efforts to make the Committee an effective force, they did not get any significant result. Benjamin said he quickly learned that a new economic proposal would not get financial support from the public unless it promised direct and immediate financial benefits to a specific group or unless it was a general emergency of great magnitude to persuade people to accept an idea or slogan that made big promises of relief, as was the case with 'Technology in the Great Depression'.

After going through the ordeal of forming the committee and getting the book published, on condition, Benjamin said every Sunday throughout the year he turned to the front page of 'The New York Times Book Review' to find out whether any significant economist was looking at 'Storage and Stability' as the principal solution to the problem of economic depression. After all, the Times had given a very favourable review of Security Analysis and this new assignment was far more important. However, he concluded that apparently the 'Times' regarded his book as just another excursion into dismal science. Though the 'Times' included the name of 'Storage and Stability' in their list of publications, but did not bother to review it. Benjamin said his dismay was deep and only partially lightened by the fact the book received notices of various lengths in several economic journals. Though these notices came at a very slow pace, he added.

Benjamin said he was very pleased when a review was published in one of the most important scholarly publications—*The American Economic Review*. In the same issue Benjamin also had his own article published on the subject. The review was written by another Graham—Frank D. Graham—who was a professor of Economics at Princeton University. The review was friendly and even enthusiastic, he added.

Benjamin said it was needless to say that Frank Graham was not affiliated with him in any manner till that time. However, the two later became very close friends through contacts following his review and Frank also became an investor in the Graham-Newman Fund.

Speaking about his book post publication, Benjamin said in the years following the publication of *Storage and Stability*, several economists from different levels of reputation, showed an interest and support in his proposal. Some of his good friends insisted that a movement should be started to popularise the CRC idea, so that it could be adopted. If ever expert global opinion settles for a new and better formulation of solid money, his idea may be accepted as the best of its kind, he added. Whereas on the other hand, he had no faith in the ability of a propaganda campaign to sell a technological idea like that of his to a major section of the public, nor did he thought that the economic policy could respond to mere popular demand was likely to make a great and favourable impression on the makers, as it had for the Townsend plan.

❑

Epilogue

Self-Portrait of Benjamin Graham At the age of 63 (May 1957)

This is the clue of his character that B has several loyal friends, very few enemies, if any. However, he never had a single close or intimate friend. Let us examine his inner life to find the answer. As a boy he was bright, charming, strange, impractical and morbidly sensitive person. He was always careful not to hurt anyone and could not understand how the other, including those who loved him very much, often hurt him out of either carelessness or malice. He began working to build a breastwork around his heart like an ottoman since very early in his life. He had accepted orthodoxy as a heaven-sent gospel.

B's character was fully formed by the last years of his adolescence, which on the surface seemed truly admirable. He had embodied all the self-promoting qualities with youthful enthusiasm like—hard-work, temperance, reliability and many other virtues. His natural kindness was reinforced by what he perceived to be a noble spirit. This was mainly because he always considered himself fortunate of his intellectual gifts. However it could also be his overzealous desire to make a favourable impression on the world. Being confident of his mental powers, he assumed that he should do whatever was honourable in order to achieve success.

B's extreme sensitivity to criticism created two traits in his character that almost marked as his specialities. The first was his tendency to avoid criticism by showing exemplary and pleasant demeanour, and the second was a basic reluctance to criticise others. His second tendency soon turned into a reluctance to even pass any judgment on them. He set before him a perfect pattern of behaviour towards the people around him, such as—he should always be polite, friendly and patient towards others; he should avoid conflicts of all kinds, even those of abstract thought, if there is any emotion involved in them.

As he grew older, he gained a measure of independence in every area in which his conscience told him that his conduct should not be dictated by tradition or prejudice alone. He became somewhat impatient with outward appearances of manners, when their result was only to deter him from following his inclinations. However, here the change was only superficial and this did not affect or reflect his essential relationship with the surrounding world.

The relationship was not as brilliantly successful as he might have wished and expected at first. A large part of the comparative failure was his treatment of women. Throughout his life he had no difficulty finding women who attracted him and for whom he had an attraction, nor was his sex life inadequate or unchanging. In his view, the only reason, which he could think of that he had troubles with women, was that they all chose to resent his good qualities, especially his balanced nature and his intelligence. Nevertheless, B in turn developed a sense of oppression and exploitation at their hands. Partly from actual experience, partly perhaps from his own imagination, he felt that almost all women were unreasonable, overbearing, ungrateful for his kindness and patience, and too insistent on entering the forbidden sanctum of his private self.

B met a woman who possessed the qualities of soul and mind, character and temperament too late in his life which he had sought in vain in many others. For her he felt that he could bring down the barriers that separated him from the rest of humanity. And for the first time he questioned the nature of these barriers under this new influence. Why, since his college, had he not accepted any man or woman into a true intellectual and emotional intimacy? Why is it so that he does not have any intimate or close friend?

Following this phase in his life, B took a fresh look at his character and what he found was not really praiseworthy. In his benevolent gestures he saw a touch of slyness, selfishness, conceit, certain artificiality and a calculated arrogance in his unwavering calmness. His third wife observed that he was humane but not human. She said he lacked true sympathy, true participation in the joys and sorrows of others. His enthusiasms were either completely impersonal like—for ideas, for artistic creations, or for things that contributed to his own growth, to his inner glory. He 'dejected praise' with unbiased modesty. However, that humility itself was expression of a pride that seemed indistinguishable from arrogance. Like Landor, he did not compete with anyone, as no one was worthy of his competence—at least in his own estimation. He recognised only one close companion, only one like-minded, he himself. His friendliness towards others was natural and unmistakable, second nature indeed. However, his first nature was remote and inaccessible to others. B finally understood it all and felt the need for less superiority and more humanity. At the age of 60 and beyond, he was to resume his emotional development. He had to accept love not as an experience of life, rather life as an experience.

Eightieth Birthday Speech of Benjamin Graham (April 11, 1974)

"Dear Malou, Brother Victor, children and grandchildren and other loved ones who are here with us, welcome to La Jolla and my eightieth birthday celebration. First of all I would like to thank my daughter Marjorie for arranging this event. Also thanks to Brother Victor for the artistic souvenir editions of some of my poems and thanks to each and every one of you for your valuable contribution to my new scrapbook.

Mark Twain, who I saw in his early youth resplendent in a white suit and curly white hair, once agreed to attend a banquet on the condition that he would not be asked to speak. However, the crowd was very insisting that at last he stood up. Very slowly and in a very mournful voice he uttered these words, "Alexander the Great is dead, Julius Caesar is dead, Napoleon is dead, and I myself am not feeling very well". And then he sat down.

Even I might say, "I am not feeling too well and I am going to sit down", however, first I have to say something.

In my eloquent, if somewhat exaggerated tribute to my father-in-law, our eminent Irving (Janice, Marjorie's husband) referred to a sketch of Ulysses which I had written a few months ago, when I was a little boy. The story and character of Ulysses made an indelible impression on me. Strange, that the Odyssey has been so important to me because the character of Ulysses is so different from my own character. He was a great warrior and a robber, whereas I have never fought with anyone in my life nor did I rob anything. He was cunning and devious, whereas I pride myself on being straightforward and forthright. Yet, it has fascinated me all my life, just as it has fascinated countless readers over the past 2500 years.

In an amateurish literary critical approach, based on a recent reading of the Odyssey, I find the story wonderful. However, poetry is mostly of a secondary standard. For one good quote as in Homer, I get twenty or more in Virgil, and so, even if I am the only man on earth to say so – Athanasius Contra Mundum (Athanasius against the world) – I will assert that Virgil is the better poet of the two.

Although where Ulysses has always been my fictional idol, there is another flesh-and-blood character after whom I have consciously modelled my life. Coincidently, we have the same first name. That person is Benjamin Franklin. He had all the qualities I aspire to—high intelligence, application, inventiveness, humour, kindness and tolerance of other's faults. Perhaps without trying, I have shared some of his weaknesses, especially for the female race. If my life can be compared even slightly with his, for both inner and outer success, I would be very happy.

Looking back at my 80 years, I am struck by a difference between the attitudes of my youth and my old age. As a youth, I was often pessimistic about my life. I found it full of mistakes, accidents and disappointments. However, I was very optimistic about the future of the world. I was convinced that with the help of science it was rapidly moving towards peace and a more comfortable existence for all. Now 80 years of pros and cons, the picture seems completely reversed. My own life has been unusually successful, even happy. However, to me the world seems to be going to hell in a horse carriage, as it was said when Sherlock Holmes went around London in a horse carriage. In today's general group thinking and group talk, ten of my grandchildren sitting on this table are expected to take responsibility for running the world when the time comes. This is a very tall order for you children to fulfil in the wonderful year 2000. I wish you success in that endeavour, but with a slight nod of the head.

Now, before I conclude, I have one final, more exciting topic to touch on. I want to say that of the pleasure I have enjoyed in life, at least half of it have come from the world of the mind, from things of beauty and culture, especially literature and art. These things are available to everyone. In fact free of charge beginnings require only a minimum of interest from us and a minimal effort to appreciate the richness spread before us. My grandchildren! If possible take that initial interest, make that continuous effort. Once you find this culture of life never let it go.

In his defence of the poet Archias, Cicero gives a famous tribute to the benefits conferred by human studies. I will narrate it, a little in Latin and then in my English translation –

Haec studia adulescentiam alunt, senectutem oblectant...
(These studies nourish our youth and comfort our age;
they adorn our prosperity and provide a refuge and
a solace in adversity; they delight us at home and
are no hindrance abroad).

Pernoctant nobiscum, peregrinantur; rusticantur.
(They spend the night with us, they travel with us, they
go to the village with us).

I have long thought that this eloquent tribute, in these same words, might also be paid to kind and lovely women in general, and especially to those whom I have known in my life – from my dear mother, who nourished my youth, to my priceless Malou, who comforts my old age. 'Pernoctent Nobiscum': more women spend the night with us, hand out with us, fart with us than our study suggests.

Now my last message! What better choice than the closing lines of Tennyson's 'Ulysses'! Words that are loved and often repeated in the Graham household –

Come my friends, 'T is not too late to seek a newer world.
Push off, and sitting well in order smite
The sounding furrows; for my purpose holds
To sail beyond the sunset, and the baths
Of all the western stars, till I die.
It may be that the gulfs will wash us down:
It may be we shall touch the Happy Isles,
And see the great Achiles, whom we knew.
Though much is taken, much abides; and though
We are not now that strength which in old days
Moved earth and heaven, that which we are, we are;
One equal temper of heroic hearts,
Made weak by time and fate, but strong in will
To strive, to seek, to find, and not to yield.

❑

Chronology

1894: Born on May 9th, London, England.

1895: Move to New York City.

1900: Begins first grade at the age of six and a half.

1901: Goes on a trip to England. Queen Victoria dies.

1903: Lives at 244, 116th Street, New York City. Attends PS 10 Grammar School. Sells *The Saturday Evening Post*. Visits various summer resorts, where father sells imported porcelain items at auction. Father dies at the age of 35.

1906: Gets admission at the Townsend Harris High School, a branch of CCNY. Studies French with Constance Fleishman.

1907: Panic in the market, US Steel fails, mother loses her entire margin account. Gets admission at the Boys High School.

1910: Graduates from Boys High, elected as class critic, summer job on farm, 'loses' Pulitzer scholarship to Columbia.

1911: Goes to CCNY, but leaves disheartened. Works on a variety of jobs—classifieds advertising salesman, move cashier, telephone assembler. Dean Keppel apologises for the administrative error, and Ben gets into Columbia on an alumni scholarship.

1912: Studies Mathematics, Philosophy, English, Greek and Music in Columbia. Works at various part-time jobs, first girlfriend, Elda Miller.

1913: Works on Hollerith card-punch and card-sort machines leased by the Calculating-Tabulating-Recording Company (later named IBM) at the US Express in Columbia. Promoted to manager, takes sabbatical from Columbia College. Publishes articles in Vogue. Teaches children of army officers at Governor's Island.

1914: Graduates from Columbia College, hold second position in Phi Beta Kappa class, decides to pursue a career in Finance on the advice of Dean Keppel. Refuses three possible teaching jobs in Columbia College. Teaches tuition to General Leonard Wood's son. Teaches English to foreign students at Bronx Night School. Stay at the luxurious Hunts Point Palace Apartments. Is invited by Carl Van Doren to become an instructor at the Brearley School, but declines. Hears Yvette Gilbert reciting a war poem. Due to anti-German sentiment, the family changes their name from Grossbaum to Graham. Joins the brokerage firm of Neuberger Henderson and Loeb. Writes an appraisal of the Missouri Pacific Railroad, which invites an offer of a safety analyst position by JS Watch and Company, but Neuberger didn't allow him to leave.

1915: Meets Hazel Mazur. Quits night school job, but continues to tutor the sons of the officers on Governor's Island. Works as a board boy in the customer's room at Neuberger's. Speculation ensues in Missouri Pacific Stock, which is condemned by Neuberger. Successful completion of arbitrage analysis of Guggenheim Exploration Company. Purchases his first car jointly with Cousin Lou. Donates his Hebbel and Lessing sets to the Columbia University Library.

1916: Announces engagement with Hazel. Salary rises to 50 dollars a week. US Express goes bankrupt. Neuberger negotiates the purchase of House Securities for the company; he also acts as the company's bookie for placing bets on the presidential election.

1917: Marries Hazel. Brother Leon also gets married. Starts an unsuccessful venture of a phonograph shop with brothers and sells it at a loss in 1919. The draft board grants adjournments. Joins the Army Reserve. Invests money for Professor Tessin and loses it in a mini-crash, then repays to Tessin at a rate of 60 dollars a month. Publishes article in *The American Mathematical* monthly magazine.

1918: Mother comes to stay with him. Tension arises between mother and Hazel. Makes a small attempt as business consultant with mother's elder brother, Maurice Gerard. Birth of their first child Isaac Newton. Writes article for *The Magazine of Wall Street* on how to determine the value of goodwill. Writes dozens of articles for this magazine in the years to come.

1919: Army reserve training ends. Does a comparative analysis of Railroad bonds. Become successful in Wall Street. The Bull Market of 1919. Loses good money in used tyres. After negative analysis of Chicago, Milwaukee and St. Paul, meets its Vice-President Robert J. Mairony, who becomes a lifelong friend and later ally. Manages successful call operations with Pierce Oil Bonds.

1920: Becomes junior partner at Neuberger, Henderson and Loeb. Makes highly successful deals in Japanese bonds with his friend Junkichi Miki. Starts a circular newsletter with the help of Leo Stern. Analyses the Tyre industry. Accepts 20,000 dollars investment from Uncle Maurice Gerard who wishes to retire and live on investment income. Becomes American citizen. Goes to live in Mount Vernon. Birth of first daughter.

1921: Recommends trading short-term US Victory Bonds for long term US Bonds and is proven correct. Considers Commodity Reserve Currency Scheme.

1922: Maurice Gerard and Graham Family moves back to New York to live near Wall Street.

1923: Leaves the Neuberger and form the Graham Corporation, a private investment account with the Harris family. Executes 'Successful Due Pont' General Motors arbitration. Buys stocks in US Express, which is now in liquidation.

1924: Goes on a ski holiday in Mayopack with Hazel and both the children, Newton and Marjorie.

1925: Dissolves The Graham Corporation as Harris moves out. Ben also disbands the Graham-Cohen account (with Benjamin V. Cohen). Ellen, his second daughter is born. Spends summer in Deal, New Jersey.

1926: Creates a new structure called 'Benjamin Graham Joint Account', in which he gets only a percentage of the profits. The investors put in 4,00,000 dollars. Jerome Newman joins the firm, then becomes a partner. Finds out the depreciation of the Northern Pipeline. Once again spends summer in Deal.

1927: Request at the stockholders' meeting that Northern Pipeline should pay surplus to the stockholders, but is defeated for lack of approval. Meets John D Rockefeller. Son Newton dies of meningitis. Starts teaching at Columbia. Meets Bernard Baruch and Winston Churchill. David Doss first becomes his student and then collaborator. Hazel goes on a trip to Europe.

1928: Wins the Proxies battle with Northern Pipeline and becomes a Director, as the company agrees to distribute additional holdings to its stockholders. Becomes Deputy Director of the unlucky Unexcelled Fireworks Company. Birth of Newton second. Goes on trip to Europe. Moves into an expensive duplex Beresford Apartments. Begins teaching the highly popular Advanced Security Analysis at Columbia and continues till 1954.

1929: Joint Account worth 2.5 million dollars; Bernard Baruch offers a partnership, which he declines. Holidays on Baruch's brother's Yacht. Agrees with Baruch that crash is imminent, however unlike Baruch leaves a portion of the portfolio in the Stock Market. The Account shows 20 per cent loss for the year.

1930: Worst fiscal year for the Joint Account, a decline of 50 per cent. There is no income from the Joint Account for five years. Makes a living by teaching, writing and consultation jobs. His marriage to Hazel begins to crumble.

1931: A decline of 16 per cent in the Joint Account.

1932: A 3 per cent decline in the Joint Account (70 per cent of the original 2.5 million dollars is gone). Chairs the protective committee to secure the proceeds of the preferred Stock in the Aeolian Record Company. Lives in less luxurious apartments in El Dorado. D Jones average is 40. Presents Commodity Reserve Currency Plan at Economic Forum at New School for Social Research. Publishes a three-part series called "Is American Business Worth More Dead Than Alive?" in the Forbes.

1933: The value of Joint Account is 3.75 million dollars, earns 50 per cent profit. Publishes articles in Economic Forum. Writes plays titled 'China Wedding' and 'The Day of Reckoning', but none of them is staged. Appears in court as an expert witness for the first time. Then appears 40 more times in the coming years.

1934: The first edition of Security Analysis is published by McGraw-Hill (later editions comes out in 1940, 1951, 1962 and 1988). Their third daughter Winifred is born. The Fund offers to pay 20 per cent of the profits directly to Graham and Newman. His play Baby Pompadour (formerly titled True to the Marines) opened on Broadway at the Vanderbilt Theatre on December 27 and closes after four performances. The Fund adopts new methods of financial accounting. The government consults him regarding the proposed Securities Exchange Act.

1935: All Depression losses have now been recovered. Helps in establishing the New York Society of Security Analysis.

1936: Changes Joint Account to 'Graham-Newman Corporation' under pressure from IRS. Meets Carol Wade on the cruise.

1937: Publishes *Storage and Stability* (McGraw-Hill) and the Interpretation of Financial Statements (Harper & Row, 2nd edition in 1955) with Charles McGolrick. Carol becomes his mistress. Proposes divorce to Hazel. When she refuses, he moves to Reno despite protests from his lawyer. Hazel finally agrees and he gets a divorce in Reno.

1938: Marries Carol at Sherry Netherlands Hotel in New York.

1940: Divorces Carol as well. A revised version of Security Analysis comes out. A lonely bachelor, he goes for roller-skating and attends Brooklyn Dodgers baseball games. He begins a relationship with his secretary, Estelle Messing, whom he later marries.

1941: Addresses the American Statistical Association in Hartford on 'A Programme to Stabilise the Purchasing Power of the Dollar'.

1942: Proposes a board of qualifiers for the New York Society of Security Analysis.

1943: Last contact with Carol Wade happens. Marjorie gives birth to first granddaughter, Cathy Janis (Later there were ten more grandchildren).

1944: Mother is murdered in a robbery while returning from a bridge game. Marries Estelle Messing. Publishes World *Commodities and World Currencies* (McGraw-Hill).

1945: Meets John D. Rockefeller for the third time at New York State Chamber of Commerce banquet. Defends the Full Employment Act before the receptive audience. Birth of Benjamin Junior. Begins writing for the *Analyst's Journal* (which later became the *Financial Analyst's Journal*), first under the pseudonym 'Cogitator' and later under his own name.

1946: Addresses Summer Institute for Social Progress, Wellesley, Massachusetts on 'Our Economic Future, its Direction and Control'. Engages in a public debate with Floyd Odium (Chairman of Atlas Corporation, friend of Howard Hughes and husband of Jacqueline Cochran) about the wisdom of buying distressed companies.

1947: Meets Dwight D Eisenhower. Speaks at the first annual conference of the Federation of Financial Analysts (later the Institute of Chartered Financial Analysts), urging formal certification exams and standards for the profession.

1948: Buys control interest in GEICO, then takes it public.

1949: Writes and publishes *The Intelligent Investor* (2nd edition in 1954, 3rd in 1959, 4th in 1973, last with the help of Warren Buffet). The Graham-Newman partnership begins.

1950: Owner of coal and railroad properties, becomes a member of the Board of the P&R Company.

1951: Serves as President of the Jewish Guild for the Blind (till 1953). Attends Columbia Graduate School of Business.

1952: Addresses the Institute of Chartered Financial Services on 'Towards a Science of Security Analysis'.

1953: Writes 'Stock Dividends' for Barren's.

1954: Appoints Warren Buffet. Graham-Newman new capitalised at 6 million dollars. A Korean War veteran travels to France to retrieve the belongings of Newton II, who committed suicide. A correspondence begins with Malou, which whom he fell in love. They spend much time together in the following years.

1955: Explains his success in deposition before a Senate Committee headed by James Fulbright. Ellen received her PhD in Psychology from Yale University.

1956: Dissolves the Graham-Newman Corporation and the Graham-Newman partnership and moves to Beverly Hills with Estelle and Benjamin Junior. He lives across the street from his cousin Roda Gerard Sarnat and her husband Dr. Bernard Sernat at 611 North Maple, where he teaches for 15 years without pay.

1957: Writes autobiographical short stories.

1958: Testifies before the House Ways and Means Committee on Dividend Policy, Margin Rules and Capital Gains Tax (which he favours to preserve).

1959: Quits tennis.

1960: Goes to his London home.

1962: His efforts to professionalise security analysts leads to the creation of the Financial Analysis Federation, later renamed the Association for Investment Management and Research, which certifies Financial Analysts by examination. Publishes the fourth edition of Security Analysis with Sidney Cottles and Charles Tatham. (A fifth edition appeared in 1988 under the auspices of Frank Block).

1963: Sits for a portrait by a Dutch painter Jan Hoovig, paid for by Buffett and other alumni and donated to the Financial Analysts Federation.

1964: Marjorie publishes A Two-Year-Old Goes to Nursery School: A Case Study of Separation Reactions (Tavistock Press). His friend's son Andrew Godman, who like Benjamin Junior is a volunteer in the Southern Voting Rights Movement, is killed in Mississippi.

1965: Resigns from the Board of Directors of GEISO.

1966: Moves to La Jolla (7811 Eads Avenue) with Malou. The two live there for a few months of the year and divide the rest of their time between Malou's home in Aix-en-Province and (for a while) at Phunchal, Madeira.

1967: Publishes own translation of Uruguayan novel *The Truce* by Mario Benedetti with Harper and Row.

1968: Warren Buffett and other former students of Graham make a trip to seek his advice on the market. They all meet at the Hotel Del Colorado. Corresponds with Adam Smith, author of 'The Money Game'.

1970: Travels to Australia.

1971: Jerry Newman resigns from GEICO's Board of Directors.

1974: Eightieth Birthday Celebrations: delivers a speech and is presented with a printed copy of his poems by his brother Victor. Lectures at Institute of Chartered Financial Analysts on 'Value Renaissance', and urges analysts to buy stock at 'fair-sale' (at 600 dollars) (excerpt from Barron's, September 23, 1974).

1975: Receives the Molodovsky Award, the highest award given by the Federation of Financial Analysts.

1976: James Buchanan sets up the Ray-Graham Fund with Ray. Dies on September 21 at Aix-en-Province, France. Malou, Marjorie and Ellen arranges for his cremation and Marjorie brings his ashes to the United States. The family holds a memorial and interred his remains at the Stephen Wise Free Synagogue Westchester Hills Cemetery in Hastings-on-Hudson, New York. A memorial service is also held at the Faculty House of Columbia University.

Benjamin Junior receives an MD degree from the University of California Medical School. With GEICO is on the brink of bankruptcy, Buffett buys heavily into it, owning 49 per cent by 1990 (and buying the rest in 1995).

1977: First wife Hazel dies.

1979: Demise of daughter Winifred Graham Downsbrow.

1981: Demise of third wife Estelle Messing Graham.

1982: Ray-Graham makes a public mutual fund.

1984: McGraw-Hill celebrates 50th anniversary of Security Analysis in Columbia. Dodd receives honorary doctorate.

1986: Warren Buffett delivers his famous speech 'The Super-Investors of Graham and Doddsville' (later published in Hermes and in the final edition of The Intelligent Investor).

1987: Death of David Dodd.

1988: Elected to the US Business Hall of Fame in Atlanta. Other laureates includes Stephen Bechtel, Andrew Carnegie, Walter Chrysler, Walt Disney, Pierre Du Pont, George Eastman, Thomas Edison, Henry Ford, A.P. Giannini, Conrad Hilton, Henry Kaiser, Henry Luce, Andrew Mellon, J. Pierpont Morgan, Adolf Oakes, William Paley, J.C. Penney, John D. Rockefeller, David Sarnoff, Alfred Salon, even Benjamin Franklin and George Washington too. The award was accepted by Benjamin Junior for the Graham Family. Robert Helbrun establishes the Professorship of Money Management and Finance at Columbia Business School as the 'Cornerstone of a Graham and Dodd Research Institute'.

❑

Reference Books

1. *Irving Kahn and Robert D. Milne,* 'Benjamin Graham, the Father of Financial Analysis'.
2. *Benjamin Graham and Rodney G. Klein,* 'Benjamin Graham on Investing: Enduring Lessons from the Father of Value Investing'.
3. *Robert L. Bloch,* 'My Warren Buffett Bible'.
4. *Benjamin Graham,* 'The Memoirs of the Dean of Wall Street'.
5. *Benjamin Graham and David Dodd,* 'Security Analysis'.
6. *Benjamin Graham,* 'The Intelligent Investor'.
7. *Benjamin Graham and Spencer Barrett Meredith,* 'The Interpretation of Financial Statements'.